T.S.   E

LADYKILLER

D1506604

LADYKILLER

Donna Fielder

BERKLEY BOOKS, NEW YORK

THE BERKLEY PUBLISHING GROUP
Published by the Penguin Group
Penguin Group (USA) Inc.
375 Hudson Street, New York, New York 10014, USA

Penguin Group (Canada), 90 Eglinton Avenue East, Suite 700, Toronto, Ontario M4P 2Y3, Canada (a division of Pearson Penguin Canada Inc.) • Penguin Books Ltd., 80 Strand, London WC2R 0RL, England • Penguin Group Ireland, 25 St. Stephen's Green, Dublin 2, Ireland (a division of Penguin Books Ltd.) • Penguin Group (Australia), 250 Camberwell Road, Camberwell, Victoria 3124, Australia (a division of Pearson Australia Group Pty. Ltd.) • Penguin Books India Pvt. Ltd., 11 Community Centre, Panchsheel Park, New Delhi—110 017, India • Penguin Group (NZ), 67 Apollo Drive, Rosedale, Auckland 0632, New Zealand (a division of Pearson New Zealand Ltd.) • Penguin Books (South Africa) (Pty.) Ltd., 24 Sturdee Avenue, Rosebank, Johannesburg 2196, South Africa

Penguin Books Ltd., Registered Offices: 80 Strand, London WC2R 0RL, England

The publisher does not have any control over and does not assume any responsibility for author or third-party websites or their content.

LADYKILLER

A Berkley Book / published by arrangement with the author

PUBLISHING HISTORY
Berkley premium edition / March 2012

ALWAYS LEARNING   **PEARSON**

I want to thank the dedicated officers of the Denton Police Department, the Texas Rangers and the Denton County Sheriff's Office for their hard work to achieve justice for Viki Lozano. My special thanks to Chief Deputy Sheriff Lee Howell for his help in researching the story, Texas Ranger Tracy Murphree for his support and prosecutors Susan and Cary Piel for their determination and courtroom expertise. Justice persevered.

PROLOGUE

It was quiet in the death room.

The crime scene team moved slowly around the king-sized bed, collecting evidence and making notes. They picked up the gun oilcan carefully. It was a good place to recover fingerprints. The oil and the rest of the gun-cleaning kit went into evidence bags. Detective Jeff Wawro unloaded the Glock model 17 pistol and put the gun and its 9 mm ammunition into separate bags. The pistol was soaked in cleaning oil. Oil dripped from the slide as Wawro worked it to eject the last cartridge. The pistol had been lying on a greasy, stained newspaper on the bed. The detective couldn't imagine his own wife allowing such a mess on such an obviously expensive coverlet.

Detectives Craig Fitzgearld and Jason Grellhesl delved through papers in the computer desk and looked for anything out of place in the small kitchenette that was part of the large bedroom suite. They found cards from Viki Lozano to her husband, Bobby, telling him how much she loved him and their eleven-month-old baby, Monty.

They moved respectfully, if a bit uneasily, around Viki Lozano's body. They knew her.

Viki's half-closed gray blue eyes seemed to follow them around the room. But she was still, lying there with her shoulder-length blond hair spilling out around her. She wore bloody pajamas, blue with little yellow ducks on them, the top perforated by a round bullet hole in almost the dead center of her chest. The covers on the canopy bed were in disarray, and part of the right side of the top coverlet lay over the leg still on the bed. A great deal of blood had spilled from an exit wound low under her left arm and onto the sheet, bed pad and mattress.

She lay on the right side of the bed with one foot hanging off, almost touching the floor. Lividity was obvious in the foot. Before the paramedics left, they said there was lividity also on her back. Lividity was blood pooling after the heart stopped. Gravity caused the blood to gather in the lowest parts of the body. It took a certain amount of time for that to happen. If things had occurred the way her husband, Detective Robert "Bobby" Lozano, had said they did, the lividity should not have been there. But he was a fellow officer in the Denton, Texas, police force. Could one of their own be lying about a crime? The detectives avoided each other's eyes.

Police detective lieutenant Lee Howell was the highest-ranking officer at the house. He noticed a pair of obviously worn white athletic socks that looked like they had been dropped in the middle of the cleaning kit from above. What were they doing there?

Howell had a bad feeling about this. A very bad feeling.

The noise of a restless child whimpering came from a speaker on the desk.

"Turn off the baby monitor," Howell told Grellhesl.

The detective walked to the desk and twisted a dial, and the noise subsided.

———

Outside the closed bedroom door, beyond the two officers set there to guard it, family members murmured and cried in the kitchen and living room. Bobby Lozano paced. Sometimes he stood at the kitchen island with his head in his hands. His sister, Blanca, hovered protectively near him. His brother Frank, a University of North Texas police officer, cried quietly as Frank's wife, Tricia, went to the nursery to comfort the baby.

A troupe of small dogs, most of them apparently of no particular breed, roamed the large living area looking for attention or curled up on the furniture for naps. The relatives absently petted them or shooed them away.

Javier, another brother, sat off to himself, obviously too distraught to speak to the others. He'd been close to Viki. Bobby's parents huddled together on a couch looking confused and anguished. The Lozanos were both from Mexico, and neither spoke a lot of English; they didn't understand what was happening. Their daughter-in-law was dead—that was all they knew.

David Farish, Viki's brother, tried to comfort his mother, Anna Farish, who was sobbing hysterically.

"Not my Viki," she wailed over and over. "Why is God doing this to me?"

Police social worker Richard Godoy tended to the family's needs while studying Bobby. Godoy had spent time with the family before. He and Bobby were good friends—Bobby had even been the best man at Godoy's wedding. But something about the detective appeared off to the experienced counselor. Bobby's face would occasionally contort, as if he were crying, but no tears appeared. When he talked about Viki, it was as though he were discussing one of his cases, not his own wife. Calm.

Godoy was puzzled. He knew what grieving people did. And didn't do.

Bobby explained to everyone who came to console him that he'd been away from the house for only half an hour, leaving his gun unloaded and ready to clean when he returned home. They planned to take Monty and go to the shooting range the next day, he said. He found Viki dead when he walked back into the house. Obviously, he said, she must've been trying to clean the gun and it accidentally discharged.

"This wasn't supposed to happen," Bobby repeated.

"It's OK," his sister, Blanca, said. "We've only got one shot at life, and we have to make it count."

Poor choice of words, Godoy thought. *What in the world was that supposed to mean?* He also was puzzled about Bobby's perfectly clean hands and clothing. Bobby said he'd tried to perform CPR on his wife. But he had not a drop of blood on him that Godoy could see.

Bobby looks like he's ready for a photo shoot for GQ magazine, as usual, he thought.

Back in the bedroom, medical examiner investigator Dwight Crawford took photographs, bagged Viki's hands in brown paper sacks and finished his notes. Funeral home attendants could take her to the medical examiner's office now, he said. Blood gushed from the exit wound as they transferred her to a gurney. She had bled internally. Blood spilled on the pristine carpet, pooling a little in fresh steam cleaner grooves.

Bobby asked to see his wife before they took her away. Crawford gave permission but told him not to touch her. They rolled the gurney to the front porch. Godoy and Detective Benny Parkey stood on either side of Bobby as Crawford unzipped the heavy plastic body bag to reveal only Viki's face. They all tensed, and Bobby's shoulders shook. He stared down at his wife, mother of his baby, dead on the day after their sixteenth wedding anniversary. He mumbled something Godoy couldn't understand. Then:

"Take care," he said to her, and he walked back into the house.

CHAPTER 1

THE DAY IT BEGAN

I was working a rare Sunday shift at the *Denton Record-Chronicle* on July 7, 2002. My seniority usually kept me from having to pull a shift on a weekend or a holiday, but it sometimes still happened. I had originally joined the paper in the features section, writing lively stories about local people who cooked special dishes, or made headbands out of rattlesnake hides, or were getting into the ostrich business. I ran contests for the ugliest pickup trucks in Denton County and the oldest gadget someone owned that still worked. Life was interesting and pleasant in the Lifestyle section.

But the newspaper's owner wanted fashion. I was clueless about fashion, and I produced a fashion section twice a year that was pure puffery. Nobody seemed to notice. The owner wanted society news. I was a cactus in that flower bed. The owner wanted to fire me, but the managing editor created a place for me, and I became the assistant managing editor for investigative reporting. I loved it. I was good at it. The police blotter became the most-read part of the newspaper, brimming with details that made the people involved in the crime real to the readers. They came to realize that these people whose houses were burglarized, who had marital problems that brought the police, who got caught with a bag of pot in their cars— these people were their neighbors.

When I became an investigative and crime reporter, the world did a hundred-and-eighty-degree turn for me, and I learned what really went on behind the polished wooden doors of some of the "nice" people in town.

When I began work that Sunday in 2002, I started with my usual routine, by checking the city jail log online, to see if anyone had been arrested for an interesting crime. Then I pulled up the daily log for the Tarrant County Medical Examiner. Denton County contracts for autopsies with the medical examiner from the adjacent county, but has its own investigators. Their office is in a small two-room suite in a Denton County building on Loop 288, a major street that half encircles the city. I had visited the medical examiner's main office in Fort Worth and looked at the shrouded bodies covered with sheets in the freezer room. I had seen toes with identification tags peeking out from under the sheets. I found it all interesting, but gruesome—and though I had been invited, I'd never quite had the nerve to watch an actual autopsy.

Once on the medical examiner's website, I selected

Denton County. I looked down the list of names of people who had died on Saturday. I paused at the notation for a Virginia Kaye Lozano, age thirty-six, on La Mancha Lane in Denton. Lozano was a fairly common Hispanic name, but La Mancha wasn't a street just anyone could afford to live on. I knew Detective Bobby Lozano lived in the elite Montecito Del Sur subdivision. Maybe it was a relative, I thought. The notation read: "Cause of death, gunshot wound." Now that was interesting. No manner of death—natural, homicide, suicide or undetermined—was listed at that point. That determination would later be the crucial element in a controversy that lasted several years.

I called Sergeant Steve Macsas, my usual contact at the police department. He wasn't at work, but I had his cell phone number. He was a little hesitant when I asked about the Lozano woman on the medical examiner's website.

"It's Bobby's wife," he told me. "We don't know what happened yet. It could be a gun-cleaning accident or suicide, but we just don't know right now."

I didn't know Bobby well, but our paths had crossed during my work at the police department reporting on crime. He typically paid little attention to me, though once I changed my hair color and he went out of his way to compliment me. *Wow*, I thought. *Talk about your bedroom eyes.*

I'd also once interviewed Bobby for a cold case story about a drive-by shooting at a fraternity house. A young woman, most likely an innocent bystander just visiting the house, had been standing outside near a fence when the shooting started. She was killed, but her killer was never identified. Years later, Bobby asked me to write a story to perhaps encourage someone to tell what they knew about the murder. We went to the fraternity house, and Bobby stood near the fence for a photograph. The *Record-Chronicle* photographer laughed afterward, noting that though the weather was Texas warm, Bobby had chosen to wear an expensive-looking black wool topcoat for the photo. He'd looked good in it.

"Bobby isn't involved, is he?" I asked.

Again, I heard a certain hesitation in Macsas's voice.

"We're just waiting for the autopsy report. We don't know," he said.

This wasn't the "of course not" that I was expecting. Still, it surely wasn't an affirmative either. I was startled that he would even hesitate when asked if a police detective might be involved in the shooting death of his wife. Macsas wouldn't tell me any more but said the police report would be available in the morning. Since we didn't report suicides at the newspaper by policy, I decided to wait until I knew more before writing anything, just in case that's how it was ultimately ruled.

If I had expected all to be revealed by the report the next morning, I was wrong. The written report had very little information except the basics. Macsas was not telling me much either. Finally, he said that word had come from the top. Until the case was resolved, there would be no information released beyond the original report. I couldn't believe it. I had always been privy to background information, the detectives' gut feelings and gossip. There was no gossip with this case. Macsas said no one save the prime investigating officers would be informed. Even the other detectives were just as much in the dark as I was.

Bobby was on leave, and no one seemed to know when he would be back. With still a dearth of information about whether it was suicide, I held off on writing a story.

I tried all my tricks to get information, but this time none of them worked. I was frustrated. Clearly something was going on, and if there was more to this than a suicide, I felt I needed to inform our readers. But I couldn't. Not until suicide had been formally ruled out. I talked it over with my editors. They concurred.

Three weeks after Viki Lozano's death, Bobby resigned from the department. Additionally, I learned, an Officer Cindy Waters had resigned as well. Now I was really in a state. I felt that I was missing something important here, and I couldn't get at the answers to the questions I had. But I kept asking them.

Finally, Sergeant Macsas said that Texas Rangers Tracy Murphree and Tony Bennie had spoken with the chief. They trusted me and thought I should be given some information. The chief agreed, and Macsas was able to tell me that Bobby was indeed a suspect in his wife's death. But he would not be immediately arrested, the sergeant said. The case would be taken to a grand jury, and if he were indicted, then I would have a story. I wasn't happy with the wait, but I really couldn't report that he was a suspect if there had been no arrest. That was our policy. Unless police obtained a warrant or formally identified someone as a "person of interest," we did not print that person's name. The policy was based on good sense. Casting aspersions on someone who had not been charged with a crime was not only unfair, but potentially libelous.

So the story of Viki Lozano's death remained unwritten for a while longer as I fretted and fumed. I felt that a big story was getting away from me and I could not do a thing about it. I did write a story about how both Bobby and Cindy had resigned, and how the police were not talking about it. Efforts to reach either of them produced nothing. I'd heard rumors that the two of them had been having an affair, but I couldn't get that confirmed on the record.

And newspapers don't print rumors.

CHAPTER 2

THE EARLY YEARS

The Lozano story didn't begin that day in July 2002 when Viki took a bullet in the chest. Nor did the story end there, or for years afterward. But that was a day that changed numerous lives and led to trouble in a police agency, trouble between judicial entities that are supposed to be allies and eventually trouble in a city that had forgotten the death of a young mother and fifth-grade teacher but was shocked into action by a single newspaper story.

Justice had been delayed but would not be denied.

Denton, Texas, was a university town with little violent crime. The University of North Texas, famous for its music school, which drew students from all over the United States, was there, and across town from UNT was rival Texas Woman's University, known for its nursing school. Initially, TWU was a women's college. Period. In 1994 male students would sue to attend and finally were allowed in the graduate programs.

It was a good city for roots, with a population of only about 70,000 in the early years of Viki and Bobby Lozano's marriage. By the time he was tried for her murder, almost twenty years later, it had grown to more than 120,000 in population. At first, it was a place where people knew their neighbors, where kids played safely in the parks, where clerks in mom-and-pop stores still knew their customers by name. The chain stores moved in over the years in malls away from downtown. Denton had only one high school in the late 1980s, and people gasped when they saw the size of the new one being built on the eastern edge of town. They'd never fill that school, people said. But they did and soon needed to build yet another high school on the south edge of town.

The two universities were the top two employers as Denton grew, and most residents either worked at the universities, for county government or for the shops and businesses along University Drive and around the square. Teaching and law enforcement were common choices for people who grew up in Denton and wanted to stay there.

This was a city where murder usually involved drugs in one way or another and regular people died in regular ways. In Denton, Texas, ordinary people often died in their beds, though not often with bullet holes in their chests.

Ordinary, fresh-faced elementary schoolteacher Viki Lozano, wife of a police detective and mother of an eleven-month-old baby boy, was an exception.

It's not that unusual for a husband to kill his wife, but rarely does his mother-in-law testify in his defense.

Anna Farish, Viki's mother, was an exception.

Virginia Kaye "Viki" Farish and Robert Cruz Lozano's July 5, 1986, wedding was held in St. Andrew Presbyterian Church. Their wedding wasn't large, and only a few friends and family attended. Blanca, Bobby's only sister, was Viki's matron of honor. Bobby's father, Sotero, was his best man. His brothers and Viki's brother were groomsmen, except for Javier, who helped Viki's grandfather perform the ceremony. Family was everything, and a proper facade counted deeply.

Viki's mother, Anna, didn't seem particularly happy about her daughter marrying a Latino. In those years, "nice girls" did not marry men of color. The two families didn't mix much after the ceremony. Viki's relatives wondered, if she had taken another groom, would the wedding have been quite so small and private? Was Viki pregnant perhaps? Oh no. Viki loved children, but Anna assured her relatives that Bobby had already told her there would be no grandchildren from their marriage. Children slowed you down, he told her. Pregnancy would make Viki fat. And that just wasn't going to happen. He was going to see to it. Viki would be thin and fit, and they would be a beautiful couple.

Bobby had attended UNT, but he dropped out when he decided to become a police officer. He graduated from the police academy the year they married and went to work as a patrol officer for the Denton Police Department. The Denton PD was smaller in those days in keeping with the lower population and university town crime rate. Murder happened, but not to "nice" people. The occasional drug deal gone wrong or fight down in the "bad" part of town were what the population expected as far as murders went.

Viki wanted to teach, and she graduated from UNT's school of education after their marriage. She also loved music and played piano like an angel. Her mother, a piano teacher, had taught her from a young age, and Viki also took on music students of her own.

———

Bobby and Viki lived with her parents at first after they were married. Later, they bought a home on Emerson Lane in the same northeast area of Denton. The house was a nice one for a young couple. But Bobby had dreams of a huge house of his own design. By the time he achieved that dream his father-in-law had died of cancer.

The family decided to sell both their homes and use the money as a down payment on the house Bobby wanted. They would share responsibility for the house payments. He drew up a rough idea of the number, size and use of the rooms. He asked fellow police detective Jeff Wawro, who had a side business as a builder, to draw up a plan. The house was more than five thousand square feet under air-conditioning. It had verandas around the back, a separate entrance for Anna's piano students and a three-car garage.

The master suite was enormous and luxurious, with a huge spa tub big enough for several people, a sauna, a shower, a standard closet, a cedar closet and a huge "wardrobe room," an office, a sitting area, a kitchenette and a second laundry room. Nearby was a workout room, though Bobby preferred working out at a gym.

Anna's suite was not as large but still contained a number of amenities not standard in tract houses. The third bedroom was for Anna's mother, "Little Mama," as everyone called her, who died not long after the house was completed.

Bobby designed no guest rooms and certainly no rooms for children, though Viki wanted a baby, and at times, begged to have a baby. Each time she pressured him for a child, Bobby bought her a dog instead. By the time she died, Viki had five small dogs that slept on the big bed with her and Bobby.

The entrance hall was graced by columns. It led to the "great room" and opened to formal living and dining rooms at the front of the house.

The kitchen featured a breakfast area and a large walk-in pantry. Behind the great room were a billiards room, a sunken bar and a theater.

The house went on the tax rolls in 1997. Though Wawro had drawn the architectural plans, Bobby chose another contractor to build the house. When Viki died, Wawro was working in Bobby's stead that night as detective on call. That made him lead investigator on the case. Anna told friends that Wawro was angry that Bobby hadn't given him the building contract and that was the reason Bobby was charged with murder. She also blamed the fact that Wawro was a Mormon for his "prejudice" against her son-in-law, theorizing that he disapproved of Bobby's lifestyle.

Regardless of how she might have felt about him initially, Anna Farish eventually came to adore her son-in-law. Not only did she insist that he was innocent, even in the face of evidence from at least five of his affairs, but the two of them continued to live together even after his indictment for murdering her daughter. She eventually even permitted Bobby to bring his latest girlfriend and her three children to live with them too.

In many ways, Anna Farish seemed to love her son-in-law more than her own daughter.

CHAPTER 3

VIKI'S FAMILY AND FRIENDS

People who grew up with Viki Lozano saw the seeds of her relationship with her husband in her own family dynamics. They remembered Viki as a happy child who lived in a stricter, more formal household than her friends. A child of a university professor father and a piano teacher mother, Viki was largely cared for by a housekeeper/nanny and was always second behind a brilliant, athletic older brother who benefited from most of the praise their mother had to give. She was a teen who was a little chubby, whose front teeth protruded so badly that she lived in headgear to straighten them and whose eyesight was terrible without her glasses. A girl who had to spend time practicing the piano while her friends were playing outdoors. A girl who was punished by grounding if she ever made less than an A on her report card.

Viki Farish matured into a beautiful woman, but in her heart she was always the ugly duckling. She was smart. She was capable. But she didn't know it, her friends felt, looking back.

Growing up, Viki had had four best friends—Robin, Lisa, Alison and Valerie. They all lived in the Nottingham Woods subdivision on either Emerson Lane or Archer Trail. Their houses were similar in size, style and facades. They all walked to kindergarten together when they were five. Later, they rode their bicycles to grade school. They played their way through Easy-Bake Ovens and Slip 'n Slides to makeup and boys.

But the girls understood that the Farishes had more money. Viki's mother, Anna Farish, had inherited a large sum. Anna Farish had grown up in North Carolina, with one sister. Her mother contracted multiple sclerosis when Anna was four years old, and they lived with relatives while her father was away during World War II. Anna later met Stephen Farish at East Carolina University, and they graduated from there. She had won a scholarship to Duke University, but an illness kept her from attending.

Stephen Farish, Viki's dad, was a teddy bear of a man who acted each year as the neighborhood Santa Claus. Viki's grandmother, Anna's mother, "Little Mama," lived with them. Although she suffered from multiple sclerosis, she was a quiet part of their lives as well.

There was a certain formality in the Farish household that made the other four little girls a bit uncomfortable when they were there. Viki's mother was OK—she smiled and was nice to them—but she wasn't like their own mothers who were apt to hug any of the five girls who came close enough and as likely to discipline any of them who might get a little too rowdy in her house. Besides, Anna Farish was gone or busy much of the time, teaching piano lessons in the semidetached room off the carport. Miss Stimson, the housekeeper, was there to clean the house, cook Viki's meals and drive her places she needed to go. The girls all came and went in one another's houses, so close within a city block, without being invited in. But at the Farish house, you knocked.

None of the other households had a housekeeper either, but all the girls loved Miss Stimson.

Alison's parents were older; her mother stayed at home, and her father was a barber. She was adopted and an only child. Valerie's parents were thought of as hippies, and she was a bit embarrassed by their back-to-the-earth ways when she was young. They picked grapes and made their own wine. Her father was a landscaper and installed lawn sprinkler systems. The others didn't seem to notice the difference in their lifestyles.

She and Viki always thought they were fat, Valerie recalled. But they were just regular kids. Their feelings of self-worth had been victim to the nation's obsession with thin women. Those feelings of not being thin enough caused problems in Valerie's life. In Viki's, they laid the foundation for disaster.

Just like Viki, Robin and Lisa had university professors for dads. Robin was an ice skater. She awoke every day at 3 A.M. and was driven to nearby Dallas for ice-skating lessons and practice. She was slim, lithe, graceful and beautiful, with long hair streaming out behind her as she twirled on the ice. Anna decided that Viki should also take skating lessons. Maybe Viki would lose some weight, or her coltish awkwardness. But Viki was not lithe. She was not graceful on skates. She did well to get around the rink without falling down, and her mother took her out of the program.

The Farishes had a pool. Viki loved to swim, and unlike on the ice, she was graceful and adept in the water. Once she reached high school she joined the swim team. And she loved horses. She rode often at a nearby riding stable, and she was never afraid, no matter how tall the horse or how spirited. In high school band she played the oboe, a most difficult reed instrument, and grew more accomplished at the piano as each year passed. She also made good grades. But somehow, her mother never seemed to see all that. No matter how hard she tried, Viki couldn't become the daughter her mother wanted.

Viki never had a boyfriend before Bobby that her friends can remember. She suffered terribly from allergies. When she was younger her teeth protruded from thumb-sucking, and for years she wore some kind of torturous orthodontic device in her mouth. She didn't wear makeup when everyone else started with lipstick and eye shadow. She was the first in the group to get her period, and she missed at least one day of school a month because, her family said, she was a "free bleeder," based apparently on her heavy periods as a teenager. Later a doctor disputed that claim.

Bobby Lozano was one grade ahead of Viki. Opinions

differ on whether they were friends in high school, but in any case, it was only after she began attending UNT that she ran into him one day and he started coming around the house. He'd been a skinny kid in high school, a nobody. But he had started working out in a gym. He had muscles. He was ripped. Viki thought Bobby was handsome, and when he joined the Denton Police Department, she thought he looked sexy in his uniform. He started training her at the gym. Her extra pounds faded. Her glasses were replaced by contact lenses. The headgear was a thing of the past. The swan was emerging, but Viki only saw the duckling she had always been.

Viki thought she was so lucky. Bobby fawned over her and was charming to her parents. He seemed only to have eyes for her, though she saw the way other women looked at him when they thought she wasn't looking. Sometimes, she wondered if he looked back when he knew *she* wasn't looking. But Bobby seemed devoted to her. He loved her. He wanted to marry her. He proposed, and she said yes.

She was lovely in her wedding dress, and happy. Bobby moved into the Farish household while Viki finished at the university. She wanted to teach children. No one was surprised. Viki always had loved children and had infinite patience with them. But Bobby had made it plain from the start that he was not interested in children of his own. She would have to make do with the children she taught. And for fifteen years, she did.

From time to time the urge to have children would become so strong that Viki would beg Bobby to change his mind. Just one baby, she pleaded. She promised him that she would watch her weight and work out and be careful to regain her slim figure after the baby was born. Bobby reacted to her appeals each time by bringing home a small dog as a substitute. The five they had at the time of her death were rescue dogs.

There were rumors about their marriage from the start. The man who had wooed Viki and won her began to neglect her. He had excuses for his frequent absences from the house they bought after Viki began teaching school. He worked overtime, he said. He joined the tactical team, and it seemed to take up a lot of his evenings. Bobby's coworkers thought he had a wandering eye—and it didn't stop with his eyes either. Some said there were huge fights when Viki would learn about one of his women. There were rumors that she kept him in line as much as she could, by controlling the money. She earned a teacher's salary. He drew police pay. Neither job was a big financial career. But Bobby learned quickly about nice clothing and expensive cologne. He loved to drive luxury cars. Once, the story around the detective squad room went, when Viki found out about one of Bobby's women, she threw all his expensive clothing out in the backyard and set it on fire.

Before long, however, Bobby replenished his wardrobe.

Bobby was driving a BMW sports model when they learned Viki was pregnant. She wanted him to get rid of the two-seater because it wouldn't hold a car seat. Bobby was angry about that, friend and police social worker Richard Godoy said. He grew even angrier when his wife suggested that they buy a Toyota sport-utility vehicle.

"He had brochures for Porsches and BMWs laid out on his desk. He didn't want an ordinary SUV, like everyone else had."

But Viki prevailed that time, and they bought a Ford Explorer.

Shortly after her death, Bobby traded it in for another BMW.

CHAPTER 4

BOBBY'S FAMILY

Bobby Lozano was the last born child of Mexican immigrants Sotero and Magdalena Lozano, the only child they had in the United States. He had four older brothers: Bill, John, Frank and Javier. He had one older sister, Blanca, who had been like a mother to him in many ways since she was old enough to be tasked with taking care of her baby brother when she was young. It was a habit that followed her all her life.

The couple came from Monterrey, Mexico, where Sotero was a semiprofessional baseball player, a boxer, a bike racer and a vocalist. His day job, though, was glassblowing, and he was recruited to the United States as a glassblower for a company in Decatur, Texas, about thirty miles west of Denton.

When that company closed, Sotero moved his family to Denton, where he worked at the Acme Brick Company. The children, who all eventually became US citizens and married Americans, grew up in the Catholic Church, where Sotero sang in the choir.

Viki was not the first woman Bobby was close to who died violently. As a detective, he'd worked on several homicides. He'd seen a lot of dead people. But murder or no, females around him had a way of dying in nontraditional ways. When he was only fourteen years old, his twelve-year-old school sweetheart, Suzie Mages, went missing. On September 25, 1977, Suzie's mother left her at a Laundromat on a Sunday afternoon with a load of clothes while she ran an errand. Suzie was gone when she returned.

The laundry was on Eagle Drive, next to a Burger King restaurant. Mary Mages, Suzie's mother, ran a natural foods store on nearby Fry Street, the heart of the University of North Texas campus. The head shops, coffee shops and bars on Fry Street attracted drifters, UNT students and even high school students looking for grown-up excitement.

Suzie was small for her age, smart and shy with strangers. Her parents didn't believe she would leave with or even talk to someone she didn't know. She was last seen buying a purple Popsicle at the Burger King. Later someone remembered seeing her talking to a man with long hair.

On October 4, 1977, Suzie's body was found floating in a water-filled gravel pit in the South Oak Cliff part of Dallas, forty miles away. She had died of suffocation from having her face shoved into mud. She had been in the water for nine days, and the autopsy could not determine if she had been sexually assaulted.

Since Bobby Lozano was known to be her boyfriend, police talked to him, but he didn't know anything about Suzie's whereabouts. Police always start an investigation with people closest to a crime victim because statistics show they most often are the ones who commit the crimes, but the Denton police sergeant in charge of the case said that he never really considered Bobby a viable suspect—for one thing, he was too young to drive, and the gravel pit was forty miles from Denton.

The case was never solved.

A few years later, when Bobby was in high school, he had a girlfriend who lived at the Cumberland Presbyterian Children's Home, a church-supported place of refuge on the south side of Denton for youngsters who left troubled homes. She lived there until her sudden death, which was ruled a suicide.

Perhaps the most affecting to Bobby was the accidental death of a baby girl. As a patrol officer on December 15, 1986, he was driving "dark and hot" to a burglary-in-progress call. All his lights were turned off, and he was speeding to the call to try to catch the burglars unaware before they got away. He was on Sherman Drive heading north. A car pulled out of Windsor Drive. The driver had not seen the speeding police car with no headlights. Lozano tried to swerve, but he couldn't avoid the car. A baby girl in the backseat died.

Other officers said he wouldn't give up the baby that night. He just kept carrying the small body around until they took it from him. He later told his friend, police social worker Richard Godoy, that the incident affected him deeply. He should have sought counseling afterward, Bobby said, but he didn't want the other officers to think he was soft. The internal investigation determined he was not at fault, and he received no reprimands.

Bobby's appeal to women didn't show so much in photographs, but in person, his manner and his utter perfection in clothing and style attracted women he wanted to impress. He was muscular, with dark hair and brown eyes that could dance flirtatiously or grow soulful. His ears stuck out a bit, and his eyebrows were a little bushy. Then he learned about waxing, and his eyebrows arched beautifully, giving him a much more polished look. It was his manner, however, that kept him in women. It was courtly, a bit old-world. Girlfriends said he made them feel like they were the only woman in the world. He seemed to be at his best in the bedroom. His words were honeyed, his passionate promises seemingly sincere. His handwritten notes were flowery silly to the average uninvolved reader. His women loved them.

His marriage to Viki didn't appear to slow down his pursuit of women, but it gave him a better wardrobe to carry on those pursuits. The family money gave him the means to buy the best. He wore Armani and Hilfiger and other top brands that cost considerably more than fellow detectives paid for the suits and ties they were expected to wear to work.

Richard Godoy, the police social worker, was a friend of Bobby's and was frequently invited over to the big house to play pool and hang out on the weekends. He saw Bobby and Viki interact and believed they had a good marriage. But he also noticed some things that made him wonder. For instance, how Bobby liked to eat at a particular small family-owned Mexican restaurant in town. He always insisted on paying. When they ate there, the proprietress made his favorite dish for him, which was not on the menu. If she was the cashier, the meal was free. She hung around the table a lot while they ate. She left when her husband noticed. Godoy thought the husband didn't like Bobby. He seemed jealous. Godoy thought the man probably had good reason.

Another thing that bothered Godoy was how Bobby lived large on his wife's money.

"I would ask him, 'Where do you get this idea that you're better than everybody and deserve all this stuff? Your family is like mine—salt of the earth,'" Godoy recalled. "He would put Viki down like she was just insignificant. When I'd confront him about an affair, he'd say, 'If you think Viki's so fine, I'll let you have her.'"

CHAPTER 5

THE OTHER WOMEN

"Please don't wear that outfit again. It does nothing for you and has no class," Bobby said. Gizelle Larson* nodded, but inside she was hurt. The outfit was new. She'd paid a fair amount for it, and she thought it was pretty. It's not like she'd bought it at Walmart, she thought. But he had such exacting standards.

"I'll buy you something nice before we go out to dinner again," he said, and his latest pretty blond girlfriend had no doubt that he would.

Larson and Bobby had met in the Denton police department in December 1991 under unhappy circumstances. Larson had bounced a number of checks. She hadn't meant

---

* Denotes pseudonym

to commit a crime, but she'd run into a bad financial situation she could not seem to get herself out of. She wrote one check for her car payment she knew would not clear her account, then another to keep her electricity from being turned off. She thought she'd be able to cover them before they made it back to her bank, but she couldn't. The penalties charged by the bank just got her deeper in the hole, and pretty soon there were warrants for her arrest.

Bobby was the detective who caught the case. Larson was running with a tough crowd, and he told her he would drop the charges if she could supply him with information about the crimes some of her friends were committing. She hated to snitch on her friends' illegal activities but needed to get out of her own troubles, so she told him what she knew.

She thought she'd pulled it off, but Bobby said that wasn't enough. He wasn't going to be able to help her with just that information. Meet him at the Civic Center Park, he said one day during a telephone call. They'd drive around and talk about it and see if there was something more she could do to get the hot check charges dropped.

"So how many guys have you slept with?" he asked, as they cruised the streets. Larson was offended. It was none of his business, she said, and he took her back to her car.

Soon he started writing her little notes, sexy cards with descriptions of what he'd like to do to her. He wanted to tear off her panties with his teeth, he wrote in one of the cards. He was a passionate lover and would make all her fantasies come true. That was the theme that emerged.

She agreed to meet him one night in Avondale Park, a

small neighborhood green in the east part of Denton. He drove her to a house on Emerson Lane, which he said belonged to a friend who was out of town.

"If you give me what I want, I'll give you what you want," he told her when they were inside the house. "If we can make love, I'll see to it that your charges are dropped."

He began to unbutton her blouse. It would have been nice to get clear of the criminal mess she was in, but it felt really wrong to trade that for sex. Even so, it didn't seem like official oppression to her. She didn't realize that he was committing a felony that could cost him his job and his law enforcement license if he were found out. Larson pushed his hands away and walked outside.

"Come on back inside," he said from the doorway. "You haven't given me enough information to clear the charges, and I'm not going to help you if you don't come back in."

Larson shrugged and started heading for the car, and he angrily drove her back to the park and let her out.

But Bobby didn't give up. He called and came by her workplace. He asked her to dinner, and she agreed, not knowing exactly why. They met several times at out-of-the-way places and drove around. He wanted sex, and he told her she might as well give in because he wasn't going to stop trying until she did, laughing as though it were a joke.

He was attentive and complimentary, and he focused on her when they were together. She felt herself falling for him, but still she resisted his advances.

One night they stopped at the city-owned North Lakes

Recreation Center. It was closed at that time of the evening.

"Let's go inside," he said. "I have keys because I work out here in the gym. All the cops do. We'll be alone in there."

"No," she said. She didn't like the idea of being alone with him in a big city building.

He asked her to meet him at 8 A.M. on Valentine's Day. He had a special present for her, he said. She agreed, and he picked her up in the parking lot at North Lakes Park. He had a special surprise for a special day, he said, and tied a blindfold around her eyes.

"Now, lie down in the seat. We'll be there in just a few minutes."

When he allowed Larson to sit up and take off the blindfold, they were parked in a private garage.

"Where are we?"

"We're at my house. That's why I blindfolded you," he said.

He lit a fire in the fireplace and poured her a glass of wine. As they sat watching the fire, she accidentally knocked over the glass. With a curse, he righted the glass and ran for paper towels to blot up the mess. Then he took her to a bedroom, where she finally yielded to him. They had sex in his bed and in the shower. He was every bit as good as he had promised.

"Here, try this on. It's your Valentine's present," he said. It was a skimpy black-and-white teddy, cut to show off her curves.

"Just as beautiful as I imagined," he said when she modeled it, and he took it off of her.

"Who is that girl with you in the picture?" she asked as they lay together in the jumble of covers.

"It's my sister," he said and reached for her again.

They left his house about 1 P.M. He dropped her off, saying he'd call on Friday.

But he didn't.

She called his office number several times in the next week, but he never returned the calls. He'd been so hot for her, she thought, but he cooled off quickly as soon as he got what he wanted. She felt sick. She had fallen in love with him, with the sexy letters and the promises and the way he made her feel like the only girl in the world. Like she was living in a fairy tale. She'd been a fool.

He finally called her after about two weeks. He needed to talk to her, he said. She was to meet him at the city library parking lot on Oakland Street. He was backed into a parking space when she arrived. He gestured for her to pull into the next space so their driver's windows would be next to each other. Don't get out, he said. We can talk from here.

"Look. My supervisor found out about us. I have to quit seeing you because you are a convict," he said.

She wasn't a convict, she thought. And she wouldn't be if he kept his promise to get the charges against her dropped. But Bobby was intent on his obvious plan to dump her.

"He's listening to me over the radio right now to make sure I break up with you."

"But I thought we were going to be together. . . ."

"I can't lose my job over you!" he said. "I'm a detective and you're a criminal. Look. Just don't tell anyone you slept with me, and I'll make sure your cases get dismissed."

Filled with shame, Larson cried as she drove home. She'd been used by an unscrupulous cop. It didn't occur to her that he had committed a crime by offering to drop the charges if she had sex and then for not telling anyone what had happened. She was humiliated. And it got worse. She never told anyone about their affair, but Bobby never helped her out in the judicial process. Gizelle Larson pleaded guilty on the check charges and was placed on probation.

And then she learned from a friend that Bobby was married. He lived in that house with his wife, she thought. That woman in the picture had been his wife, not his sister. She had been such a fool.

She ran into him at a baseball game one night. "So, how's your wife?" she asked sarcastically.

"Look, we fight all the time because I want a baby and she doesn't. But I can't divorce her. I would lose too much," he said. "There's a lot of money, and I'm not going to give it up after all I've been through with her."

"But why did you lie to me? You hurt me so badly. How could you do this to me?" she asked, tears streaming down her face.

Bobby looked at her coldly.

"You did it to yourself," he said. "I didn't do anything wrong."

He walked away from her, leaving her sobbing in the parking lot.

Angie Tatum* officially met Bobby Lozano at the gym in December 1992, though she'd seen him before, around the squad room in the criminal investigation division of the police department, and he'd seemed nice. The reason she'd been in the squad room, however, had been far from nice.

Tatum had been sexually assaulted, and the crime had put a terrible strain on the petite blond woman's marriage. She just couldn't trust anymore, and she couldn't feel close to her husband. She'd changed tremendously. He'd changed too, she told police. She felt it was as though being kidnapped out of a parking lot and raped had demeaned her in his eyes. Like it was somehow her fault.

Her husband had stuck by her during the trial, when she'd had to endure telling a roomful of people what her rapist had done to her. She'd had to give embarrassing details, first to the police, then to the prosecutors in the case and then to anyone who happened to wander into the courtroom while she was being questioned on the witness stand. When it was over and her attacker went to prison, she was grateful. But the damage had been done, and she didn't think she could fix her marriage. She wasn't even sure she wanted to.

When Tatum ran into Bobby at the gym—which she went to not only to keep in shape but also to get rid of

* Denotes pseudonym

stress—they started talking, and she at last felt her bottled-up emotions begin to come out. He was a good listener. He was a strong shoulder to cry on. Eventually, he was her lover, and he was good in bed.

Tatum left her husband in April 1993, about the time she began having sex with Bobby. The divorce really wasn't because of Bobby, but it made their meetings a lot easier and less risky.

It was a casual thing. He didn't tell her what to do or what to wear. There were no impassioned letters or cards, no gifts. They mostly met in her apartment, and he never spent the night. She knew he was married, and he had told her from the start that he would never leave his wife, Viki. They argued a lot, he told her, because Viki wanted a baby. He didn't. He said they didn't have sex often, but he wanted to stay because her family had money. That was obvious, Tatum thought. He was so vain about the way he looked, about the expensive clothes he wore, about the car he drove. He wanted nothing but the best.

Tatum moved out of town in 1995, but she and Bobby still talked occasionally on the telephone. They began meeting again in 1997. She rented a motel room in Denton, and he visited her there. Bobby was odd about birth control. She knew his wife used it, but he didn't want Tatum to use anything. It was like he enjoyed the idea that she might become pregnant. Then she did. Almost immediately, however, she miscarried. She was relieved. She didn't want a child just then, but she did feel badly, and she tried to figure out just what Bobby's feelings were about it. Bobby never wanted to talk about that, and soon he ended their relationship. Angie Tatum thought it was because she'd gained weight.

———————

Why wasn't Bobby answering her page?

Liz Daley* put his number into her pager and used their "911" code to let him know he really needed to call her. She'd done it already three times, but he hadn't responded. Her face hurt like hell. She could feel the swelling; her head felt bigger than a basketball. Her face was going to look so bad, and there was nothing she could do about it.

"Miss, we really need to stitch your chin up now," the nurse said. "Can you just put down the phone?"

She'd been practicing with her softball team. The hitter connected hard with a fastball, and before she could catch it, or duck, it had hit her in the jaw. They said she hadn't lost any teeth, but her jaw was broken and she'd need surgery. Right now, she needed Bobby, but she couldn't get him.

Daley paged him again when she went home that night. Still no response. She went into surgery the next day not knowing where he was or why he wasn't there for her when she needed him.

Back in her apartment the next day, she called him at work.

"Where are you? Why haven't you called me? I got hit

———————

* Denotes pseudonym

with a ball and it broke my jaw and my face is all messed up," she said. "I need you. Please come over."

There was a long pause, and she thought he'd hung up. "Bobby?"

"I'm here. I'm sorry. I heard about you getting injured. Liz, I just can't stand to see you in that condition. It would hurt me too much. I'll come by in a week or so when you're feeling better," he said and hung up the telephone.

It was more than two weeks before she heard from him again, but he came bearing roses and told her how much he missed her, and pretty soon they were making love again.

Daley was attending college and working at a Denton hotel when she met Bobby in 1993. He and another detective, Benny Parkey, came to the hotel to investigate a report of credit card abuse she had turned in. Bobby looked deep into Daley's eyes as he questioned her while Parkey took notes. He was charming. And he definitely seemed interested in her, she thought.

She looked up from the hotel switchboard four days later, and there he stood again, smiling at her. Parkey wasn't along this time, and Bobby wasn't there about the stolen credit card. He chatted with her for half an hour. He talked about taking her to dinner.

"Are you married?" she asked. She suspected he was, even though he didn't wear a ring.

"Well, yes. But that wouldn't keep me from taking you out to dinner."

Daley knew better than to get started with a married man. But just one dinner wouldn't hurt anything, would it?

The relationship lasted four years. A novel would have called the affair "stormy." They fought often, and it always ended with her in tears.

"I like to see you cry," he told her once. "I want to see your raw emotions."

Bobby had a temper. He was jealous. He didn't want her going out with other men, and he didn't want her hanging with her friends at clubs. But Daley was social, and it didn't seem right for her to sit home alone when he was with his wife. He made her stop smoking. He complained if she drank alcohol. He took her to the gym. He wanted her to weigh a hundred and twenty-eight pounds, he said. He weighed her every time they worked out together. If she had gained a pound, he was angry and made her work out all the harder. Her resentment grew.

He brought her clothing that he insisted she wear, even though she thought it was too "old" looking for her, a college girl in her early twenties.

"I want someone with class," he'd say, and she would agree to put on the expensive outfits and the jewelry he bought her.

Daley got pregnant early on. She went to a friend's house and called him to come over. When he walked in the door she was crying. His face froze when she told him about the baby.

"You will have to take care of it," he said.

She agreed. A baby would complicate her life, and she wanted to graduate and get a job. That night, however, she miscarried.

"Someday I want us to have a child," he told her when he found out. "I want you to have my baby boy."

Daley was an education major. She told Bobby she needed to have classroom experience evaluating a teacher. The next time she saw him he had news that shocked her.

"I talked to Viki. I told her I knew this college student who needed to attend a class. She agreed that you could observe her class," he said. "You can just go in and pretend you don't know me well and watch her teach. She really is a good teacher, I think."

Daley was uncomfortable sitting at the back of Viki's fifth-grade classroom. But she had to admit that she was curious about Bobby's wife, and Viki was so nice to her that it was easy to imagine she was just another part of Daley's education and not her lover's wife. Still, she thought it was strange that Bobby would want her to meet his wife. Viki was really pretty. She had gray blue eyes and blond hair about the color of Daley's own, but not as long. She was slim and funny, and the kids seemed to love her. Viki was a good teacher. Daley could have liked her, she thought, if she wasn't having an affair with her husband. If she didn't covet him for her own. If she wasn't planning and plotting to take him away.

Viki was bulimic and suicidal, Bobby claimed. He'd caught her with his gun once, he said, and she told him she wanted him to end her life. She often told him she didn't want to live anymore, he said.

The story didn't jibe with the lively, enthusiastic teacher Daley had seen in the classroom.

Bobby and Viki were planning to build a grand house in the exclusive Montecito Del Sur subdivision of Denton that year. He talked about his dreams and plans a lot. He knew exactly what he wanted, and another detective, who built houses on the side, drew the design plans. It was going to have more than five thousand square feet, he told her. He and Viki would have a whole wing to themselves, like an apartment almost. They'd have their own kitchen area and an office and laundry room and a huge walk-in closet, plus two other closets all to themselves. There was a sitting area under the windows that looked out on the street. He planned an elaborate bath with a sauna area, a separate potty room and shower and a huge, round spa tub in black marble. Bobby's eyes glittered when he talked about that house. His mother-in-law, Anna Farish, would have her own wing that was almost as nice, and her mother would also live there in the third bedroom. But Viki's grandmother was in bad health, and he didn't think she'd live there very long. When Viki's mother was gone they'd own the house and live there without a passel of relatives, he said.

He talked about the house a lot as he and Daley lay in bed after lovemaking. He seemed obsessed with it. They'd have a three-car garage. He wanted formal living and dining rooms and a "great room" where they could entertain. Anna would have a room to teach her piano students on the other side of the house with a separate entrance. Viki had piano students now too, and she made extra money that way. When Anna was dead, Bobby said, Viki would have a lot of piano students and maybe could stop teaching school.

Daley didn't think Bobby sounded like he was going to leave his wife anytime soon.

In 1996, Daley graduated. She knew, despite all his promises, that Bobby was not going to marry her. She decided to take a few months off and travel. At the end of her vacation, she had made her decision. She wasn't going back to Denton. She wasn't going back to Bobby. She moved back to her hometown and soon began dating a former boyfriend again.

At one point, Daley cleaned out a closet. She pulled out a batch of cards and letters from Bobby and read some of them again. They sounded like something out of a romance novel, she thought. She read his fantasy about their "timeless encounter." *Wrong*, she thought, and threw the letters into the fireplace, where they quickly turned to ashes.

Liz Daley got a call from the Texas Rangers after Viki died. They wanted her to come in and give a statement about her affair. She didn't want to do that. She was afraid. She eventually agreed, but she didn't want Bobby to know.

"Whenever Bobby was dealing with a situation where he felt like he might have been wronged, he always made it very clear that he would get back at the person responsible for wronging him," she wrote at the end of her statement. "For that reason, I am concerned that he will find out that I have been interviewed and seek retaliation."

Amber Lansing's* daughter was one of Viki Lozano's piano students, and she thought Viki was doing a wonderful job. She dropped her daughter off at the big house, sometimes marveling that a teacher and a cop could live in such a place. But she had heard there was family money.

Viki's husband, Bobby, occasionally had business near Lansing's office, and he would drop by unexpectedly and sit down uninvited. It made her slightly uncomfortable. She was married and had no interest in him.

One day he dropped by with photos he wanted to show her of him and his dad on a fishing trip. After the first few, the rest were of Bobby shirtless, posing for the camera. Lansing shuffled through them and handed them back.

"Very nice," she said.

"So tell me, do you and your husband like to do it with the lights on or off?" he asked her.

"Bobby, get out of my office," she said. "And don't come back."

———

Karen Algrim was on her way out. She'd lost faith in Bobby's promises that never came true. She'd lost faith in the fantasy life she thought she was going to live with the man who gave her presents, who sang love songs to her in Spanish, who said they would soon be wed. She didn't believe him anymore. Too many broken promises, too many lies. She was about to graduate from the University of North

———

*   Denotes pseudonym

Texas, and she was leaving Denton. She wanted to find an unattached man who would love her truly and not just two days a week. She hadn't told Bobby yet, and she thought about how to do it as she watched him walk around her apartment after a bout of lovemaking. He really did have a beautiful body, she thought, his skin an even brown like a dark tan, his muscles so defined from hours at the gym every day.

Then he sat on the foot of her bed, naked, his perfect physique glistening with the sweat from their exertion.

"Something has happened," he said. "Something terrible."

His eyes welled with tears. "Viki has leukemia."

Algrim couldn't believe it. Bobby's wife was young. She knew Viki worked out and ate healthy, just as she did at Bobby's insistence. How could she be that sick?

"The doctors have given her only six months to live," he said, and his shoulders heaved and tears ran down his cheeks. "I haven't wanted to tell you, but she's very sick now, and I'll have to take care of her."

Algrim moved to comfort him. She wrapped her arms around him and crooned. What did you say to a man you were having an affair with when his wife was dying?

"I'm so sorry," she murmured, but he didn't seem to be aware that she was even near him. He got up and pulled a bottle of water from the refrigerator in her tiny kitchen. The one-bedroom apartment was small, but she had decorated it beautifully, and he often brought presents that fit the décor. He sat back down on the bed, then pulled himself up against the pillows. She nestled next to him.

"She's been begging me to kill her. The treatments are so hard on her. The nausea, the weakness. Sometimes she can barely stand," he said, tears still tracing down his cheeks. "Her hair is falling out now, and she says she just wants to die and get it over with."

"She doesn't really mean it though. You know she doesn't."

"I thought about doing it. I took some poison out to the lake and gave it to a couple of dogs to see how bad it would be. It was awful," he sobbed. "They really suffered before they died. I couldn't do that to her, no matter how hard she begged."

Algrim held him as he cried. "Of course you couldn't do that."

Bobby stopped crying, and his mood lifted. He began to talk about the money. He'd taken out a million-dollar life insurance policy on Viki, he said. At least when she was gone he'd have money. Viki had cut Bobby out of her bank accounts a couple of times when she was angry, he'd told her. He hated to be controlled by her money. In a couple of years he'd have the trust that her father had set up for him. Viki couldn't control him then, Bobby said. Algrim didn't know how to reply to that. Years later she learned that the trust fund was another lie—or wishful thinking.

They'd met the first day she came to work as an intern at the Denton Police Department. Karen Algrim was in the social work program at the University of North Texas, and an internship was part of the curriculum. She worked with police social worker Richard Godoy. He was a nice man, and she knew she would enjoy being in the busy department where he counseled people in marital crisis whose lives the police had entered via a 911 call. Godoy was also called out when death, be it accidental, natural or homicidal, came to visit. He was good at comforting people, and Algrim thought she could learn from him.

Bobby walked into Godoy's office that first afternoon to welcome her. Then he handed her his card with an invitation to call him if she needed anything. He had bedroom eyes, she thought, noticing that he'd written his pager number on the back of the card.

He dropped around the office often, and soon he asked her out. But she'd checked with one of the women at the department. Bobby was married, and she didn't want any part of that. "No" only seemed to make him more determined. Couldn't they just go for a drive and talk? Finally, she agreed to that. They drove to the Las Colinas area of Dallas, sat on a bench in front of the statues of mustangs racing through the area and talked for hours. A few days later he asked her to dinner, and she accepted. After that, they went to many dinners and several movies. And one night, she allowed him to come into her apartment. He wanted sex, but she said no.

"You're the first woman to ever tell me no," he said. "I can't believe it."

"No" didn't last for long, though. He just never let up. And when she finally said yes, she learned that he was indeed a passionate, thoughtful lover who thrilled her like none other in her limited experience with sex. She wanted to marry Bobby, and he said he wanted to marry her too.

But he never left his wife. He lived with her in a huge,

fancy house in one of the best neighborhoods in Denton. His mother-in-law lived there too, Algrim knew, in a separate wing of the house. He'd told her all about his plans for the house, including the big, round black marble spa tub and the massive wooden front door he planned to order from Mexico.

Bobby introduced Algrim to his sister, Blanca, who knew they were having an affair but didn't seem to care. Algrim took that as a good sign. If he wasn't worried about his family knowing about her, surely that meant that he planned to leave his wife soon. The infrequent trips to watch him play in a baseball league were different. She was uncomfortable there, sitting with wives and girlfriends of the other guys while he was on the field. They didn't talk to her much, and she knew they knew he was married. But he seemed to flaunt her to the other guys, and he insisted that she go with him to some of the games.

He wasn't ashamed of her, or any of the other women he talked about. Early in their relationship he told her about the week of his wedding. He'd been with another woman the day before his marriage, he told her, and with a different woman the day after. Sometimes, he said, he'd rent a hotel room and have as many as three women meet him there one after the other, timing their entrances and exits carefully.

"But that was before I met you," he insisted. "I was bored with every relationship, and I wanted to move on. But you have changed all that," he would tell her over and over. "You have changed me. Now, I want only you and I can't wait for us to be together full time."

Bobby was jealous. He didn't want Algrim going out with friends, especially male friends. They fought once when he showed up and smelled cigarette smoke in her hair.

"You know my last girlfriend cheated on me. It started out just like that, just drinks in a club," he snarled. "I can't stand to think of you in one of those places with other men. I won't stand for it."

Bobby explained away his temper tantrums as a side effect of the steroids he was using to promote muscle growth, he told her. He lost his temper more easily when he was being injected with the drugs, something people called "roid rage." He would stop soon, he said. The drugs were illegal, and he could lose his job or even go to jail if anyone found out. He just needed to keep the muscles pumped.

She asked him one night how he could leave her and go home to his wife. It must be hard, she said.

"I love Viki, but I'm not in love with her," Bobby said. "We don't have a sex life. That's all over with. But she's unhappy about my being gone so much. One time she caught me having an affair and she threw all my clothes out in the backyard and set them on fire. It's really hard on me," he said. "Every time I leave her she's crying, and every time I leave you, you're crying."

It occurred to Algrim that Bobby actually enjoyed seeing women cry.

About midway through their affair, Algrim learned she was pregnant. Bobby never wanted to use any kind of birth control. She waited for him to arrive on a Friday night, and then she told him, a little afraid of what he was going to say. But she thought he might be happy, since they talked a lot about having children together. Bobby said he didn't want to have children with Viki, but he couldn't wait to have a child with her. He had a name picked out for their first son. It would be Montgomery Cruz Lozano. They would call him Monty for short.

But this wasn't the right time, Bobby said when she told him. He couldn't marry her yet, and he didn't want his child to be born illegitimately. They would have to get an abortion.

Algrim agreed. She really wasn't ready to be responsible for a child either. She wasn't finished with college yet, and she wasn't that sure at this point that Bobby would ever marry her.

On the night before the abortion was scheduled, he lay with his head on her stomach in the bedroom of her small apartment. He sang to the baby, calling it Monty and talking to it as though he weren't about to kill it, she thought, shocked and a little sickened. The next morning he took her to Dallas and paid for her abortion.

Things didn't seem to be the same after that. Algrim finally told him she was planning to move away as soon as she graduated. He cried. He begged her to stay. But she found a job in another part of Texas. She told him not to come back to the apartment he had visited so many times.

And that's when the telephone calls began in the middle of the night. No one said anything, but she knew it was him.

"I've called the police and they're checking my line," she said to the empty phone line one night.

And the calls stopped coming.

Karen Algrim moved on with her life. She found a job, and she found someone to love. She married and had two children.

A friend sent her an e-mail two years later. It contained Virginia Kaye "Viki" Lozano's obituary. She was survived by an eleven-month-old son, Algrim read. His name was Montgomery Cruz Lozano. She ran into the bathroom and threw up. Then she found all the passionate love letters she'd not been able to destroy. She threw them in the trash.

Viki had not died of leukemia. She had been shot. Algrim wondered why Bobby would bother to make up a story about his wife having a fatal disease. What was he actually doing all that time when he said he was taking her for treatments?

Bobby may not have been crying crocodile tears when she left him, but he already had another girlfriend lined up. Three months before Karen Algrim left town, Bobby had started working out with another detective at the Denton Police Department. She was also a blue-eyed blonde, just like the rest of Bobby's girlfriends. Her name was Cynthia Waters. He called her "Sin."

CHAPTER 6

SIN

Cindy Waters and Bobby Lozano were so focused on each other, so engrossed in their lovemaking, so in tune to the sounds of each other's labored breathing that they didn't hear the door. They did hear the gasp as Bobby's sister, Blanca, walked into her bedroom and saw them there in her bed. They scrambled for the covers as she hastily retreated to the living room of the small apartment.

"I didn't know you were going to be here," she said, and Bobby, almost at the same time, managed, "I didn't know you were coming home so soon."

Blanca knew her brother used her apartment. Still, it was embarrassing for them to be caught in flagrante like that. Bobby held Cindy's hand under the covers as he tried to hold a casual conversation with his sister, who stood in the next room out of sight. Cindy kept quiet. There wasn't anything for her to say.

"I'll just go to the store for a while," Blanca said. "I'll be gone about an hour if that's all right."

They heard the door close behind her, and Bobby moved close to Cindy again. He began to caress her, but Cindy was definitely not in the mood anymore.

"I need to go home," she said. "Please tell Blanca I'm sorry."

"We need our own place," he murmured in her ear. "Soon we'll have our own house and our own bed together. It will be all our dreams come true. We'll make love all day, and nobody will break in on us."

"When, Bobby?" she asked. "When is that going to happen?"

Cindy was a single mother of two young boys, a blue-eyed blonde with a figure fast approaching Bobby's idea of perfection. She had been several pounds overweight after her second baby was born. Bobby offered to help her get back in shape, and they began working out together at the gym. Bobby was a hard taskmaster as they lifted weights and toiled on the cardio machines. He made her tell him what she ate each day and disapproved of most of it. They began eating lunch together, healthy food and not too much of it. The weight started melting away. His idea of her ideal weight was a size four. She had been thinking size ten.

Her friends began telling her she was losing too much weight. She looked sick, anorexic. But Bobby liked her that way, so she continued to diet and work out with him at the gym. He could tell if she gained even a pound, and he worked her out harder than ever.

She had first noticed him when she was still married, still in uniform and he was already a detective, wearing his Armani suits to work and flashing his dark Latino eyes at her. Then she moved into the criminal investigation division of the police department as a child abuse detective. And they began to talk around the squad room. With her marriage faltering and the stress of a special needs child and a newborn always present, it was nice to have someone to take her mind off her problems, someone who flattered and flirted. Her older son was born with a hole in his heart and mild mental retardation. Caring for two little boys while she also worked was sometimes exhausting, but she found that time spent with Bobby revived her zest for life.

They talked about their marriages. She told him that she and her husband would get a divorce if they could afford it. All that was holding them together now, she said, was the lack of money needed to operate separate households.

Bobby said his marriage had been over for years, but they stayed together somehow. They were friends, he said, but not lovers. They had talked about an amicable divorce, he said. One of these days he would leave.

Bobby admitted to having had several affairs. All Cindy's friends warned her to stay away from him. Bobby was trouble. He never was without a girlfriend, and he flaunted them to the other officers. He was a player. He was no good. He made promises, they said. But he was never going to leave his wife. Her family had money, and Bobby had expensive tastes.

But he had a courtliness Cindy had never experienced. He opened doors for her. He complimented her. He sang her romantic songs in Spanish. They grew closer, and he began to speak to her of love. Bobby's eyes bore into hers as he leaned over her at the gym. His lips were close. Cindy wanted to kiss him, but they were both married to other people. It wouldn't be right.

She drew farther away from her husband as she got closer to Bobby. She was falling in love, she knew. And Bobby began pressing her for more. He loved her, he told her. He wanted to fulfill her dreams of ecstasy as no other man ever had. Cindy resisted, but she didn't want to. And one day she stopped resisting. Soon they were lovers. And it was wonderful. Bobby had a way of focusing just on her, and it was so different from most men, who turned on a ball game when the sex was over. Bobby held her and talked of them being together and waited to be ready for the next round of sex.

Finally, she knew that she had to leave her husband. She wanted a life with Bobby. So she made her break . . . but Bobby couldn't seem to manage his.

Time moved quickly after Cindy's divorce was final. She had two little boys to care for and a demanding job. Bobby spent a great deal of time at her house. He told his wife and mother-in-law he was working overtime with the tactical team. He asked to be transferred from general investigations into the family services unit where Cindy worked. They rode together a lot. Many of her cases involved Hispanic families, and Bobby was able to translate for her. Often, she made dinner for him at night. Bobby was meticulous and demanding. As soon as the meal was finished, the kitchen had to be cleaned. No dirty dishes in the sink, ever.

Cindy's hair was long down her back. Bobby asked her to cut it a little shorter and style it differently. He wanted it a little lighter too. She did as he asked, and he paid for it. Cindy had never met Viki. She would have been surprised to learn that her new hairdo was just like that of Bobby's wife. Cindy's eyes were bluer than Viki's more gray blue color, and she had a bigger smile. But in many ways, under Bobby's firm hand, they looked alike. As Bobby's other girlfriends had looked a lot like his wife.

He bought Cindy clothing now that she had lost forty pounds and her older outfits were much too large. He bought her a leather jacket. He bought jewelry—earrings and watches—and he bought her an amethyst and diamond ring. Soon, he said, he would replace it with a wedding ring.

A strange thing happened one day. Her purse was stolen. It held the expensive ring, one of the nice watches and a couple of pairs of earrings he had given her along with her wallet. She wasn't sure how the purse disappeared, but it never turned up, and no one ever tried to use her credit cards.

They talked about houses, where they would live when they were married. Maybe they would build, he said. They went house shopping and looked at homes in the $300,000 to $500,000 range. Way above their police salaries, but Bobby had money in a Mexico bank, he told her. He said he'd made it working as a bounty hunter, and his wife didn't know it existed.

One day he dropped a bombshell—Viki was pregnant. She'd always wanted a baby, and now, fifteen years after their marriage began and years after their love ended, she was going to give birth. Bobby was disconsolate. Their plans would have to be put on hold, he told Cindy. He couldn't leave his wife while she was pregnant. He would have to wait until after the baby was born to get a divorce. Cindy understood. It was hard taking care of little ones alone. Bobby's wife would need his help at first. Maybe as long as a year. A year was a long time to wait, but Cindy was willing. One day she would be Bobby's wife.

Viki's life was endangered by the pregnancy, Bobby said. She had a bleeding problem, and the doctor feared she would die during childbirth. And when the baby was born, Bobby said it had been touch and go. There had been tearing. Viki was assigned to bed rest, and he would have to care for the baby for a while.

Cindy had a big heart. She looked at her little boys and remembered how difficult things were when her older son had been born with a heart defect. She had to be patient. Bobby gave her a photo of himself and the baby sitting in the huge spa tub in the bedroom suite of the big house where he and Viki lived with Viki's mother. Once he asked her to meet him at Blanca's apartment. He brought the baby and handed him over to Cindy. Bobby was very proud of his little boy. He wanted them to have a "family" portrait made with the two of them, her two sons and Monty. Cindy was shocked. That would just not be right, she told him. She refused to pose for the portrait.

The year turned over to 2002. The months could not fly by too quickly for Cindy. When Monty was a year old, Bobby promised, he would leave his wife and they could be married.

The baby was eight months old in April when Bobby told Cindy that Viki had been to a Dallas lawyer and filed for divorce. It was going to be amicable, he said. He would walk out of the house with nothing but his clothes. But he would be walking to her, so he didn't mind. He told her he couldn't wait for that to happen.

She pressed him daily for news of his separation from his wife, and within a few weeks he told her that he too had visited the lawyer. Both of them now had signed the papers, but they had not been filed. He said that Viki had asked him to stay until school was out. She was planning to take the next year off from teaching so she could stay home with Monty. Viki was excited about it, and would take on more piano students to help with the money. They planned for him to move out June 30, he said. They were waiting for an opportune time to tell their parents.

"She's been in touch by e-mail with an old boyfriend," he told Cindy. "They might get back together." He was pleased that everything seemed to be working out.

On the first weekend in June, Bobby and Cindy were supposed to have dinner with his parents to give them the news and then tell Viki's mother the next day. Bobby came to Cindy in exasperation. Family was coming in from

Mexico that weekend to stay with his parents. He couldn't tell them with extended family around.

Cindy began to have a funny feeling in the pit of her stomach. Was this breakup really going to happen?

They gave Anna the news that Sunday, Bobby later told Cindy. Anna had known it was coming and wasn't too upset.

"If you want me to I'll move into a hotel right now," he said.

But Cindy said no, he should wait until he could make a permanent move.

Bobby was even more upset the next weekend when he told her that he talked to his parents. His mother was horrified. She cried. She begged him to work things out. She told him he could not move in with them.

"She said she wasn't going to help me get a divorce," Bobby said.

Cindy was distraught. He would not be moving this weekend. The bad feeling in her stomach grew stronger. She checked the court records for a divorce filing. She didn't find one. Bobby explained that Anna was embarrassed about the divorce and had paid an extra ten thousand dollars to have it sealed.

But Bobby said not to worry. He'd rent an apartment. And later he called to tell her he had an apartment, but he still had to wait until June 30 to leave because the apartment wasn't ready.

"I know I'm doing the right thing," he told her. "I don't want Monty to grow up in the tension that is in our house right now. But I want him to know that he is loved."

The next weekend was Father's Day. Bobby said that Viki and Anna Farish were going to be out of town on a piano recital trip. He would spend the weekend with her, he told Cindy. Her boys would be with their father. Bobby bought tickets to a water park for the two of them. Rarely did she get to spend this much time alone with him. Cindy was excited.

But Thursday came, and Bobby had bad news.

"My father's brother has been badly injured in a car crash in Mexico," he told her. "My father's too upset to drive, and his health is not good enough to make the trip by himself. I'm going to have to fly down there with him."

Cindy agreed that there was nothing for him to do but make the trip. They were flying out Friday morning on American Airlines, he said. She tucked the water park tickets away.

Bobby asked her if she would help him with a job issue. He was supposed to arrest a man that Friday on a warrant. The man was about to rabbit, he said. Would she get together with the INS officer he was working with and make the arrest? Cindy took care of it for him.

He didn't call on Friday, which was unlike him. Usually, he called her several times a day. He didn't call Saturday. The detective in her smelled a rat. Cindy and her best friend were taking their children to the lake on Saturday before their father picked them up for visitation. On the way, she drove by Bobby's house. There was no indication that anyone was at home. She drove by his parents' house. It was quiet there too. On the way home from the lake she made the route again. Still no one home at either house.

Blanca called on Sunday. Bobby had phoned her and asked her to tell Cindy that everything was all right, she said. How was her uncle? Cindy wanted to know. When was Bobby coming home? Blanca was evasive. She said that Bobby hadn't really said much. He was in a hurry. Blanca hung up soon after that. Cindy's suspicions rose. Why not call her himself? Why have his sister relay a message? What in the world was going on?

She called the airlines and checked on the time Bobby had flown out Friday. They could not find his name on a flight list. What about a flight home Monday? She asked. No, no Lozano had reservations Monday either. On Monday morning she drove by Bobby's house again. Still no sign of anyone at home. But when she passed the elder Lozanos' house, she saw his father outside mowing his lawn. Bobby was lying. She knew it now. She just didn't know why.

One of the other detectives suggested that the department send flowers to Bobby's uncle in Mexico. Cindy said she'd find out where he was hospitalized. She called Bobby's father to find out. He didn't know, the old man said. He wished he could see his brother, but he wasn't in good enough health to travel. Clearly, Bobby had taken a real event and magnified it to use for an excuse to scuttle their plans. Why did he need his father for the lie? He could just as easily told her that he was going alone to visit the uncle, but Bobby liked details in his fabrications.

Bobby showed up at Cindy's house Monday night. He'd heard about her telephone call, and he admitted he had lied. He'd needed to care for Monty while Viki and her mother were busy with the piano recitals, he told her. He'd been with his wife and mother-in-law all weekend. He was so sorry that he'd broken Cindy's trust, but he'd wanted to be with his small son on Father's Day.

"I could have handled anything better than a lie," she told him. "As far as I'm concerned, it's over between us. You are never going to leave Viki, and I just need to move on with my life."

Bobby cried. He begged her to forgive him. He begged Cindy not to give up on their love, their life together. He told her he'd never loved anyone like he loved her and that he would rebuild her trust if she would just give him another chance. He knew what he had to do, she told him. She would never believe he was leaving Viki until he actually left.

"I know I let you down," he pleaded. "And if I haven't moved out by June 30, then I will know that you have nothing to believe in, and I will walk away. But just give me a little more time. Give me this one more chance."

———————

Viki was quietly happy in those months of spring and early summer of 2002. Things were looking up. What she had wanted most was more time with her long-awaited son, and now she had plans to stay home all next year with Monty. She was planning a birthday party for him in August. Her schoolteacher bent for decorations and programs was pushing her over the top with party ideas. But after all, how often do you get to see your firstborn become a year old?

It had been hard saying good-bye to her teacher friends

at the end of the school year. She gave away most of her classroom decorations when she was packing up on the last day of classes. She'd gotten a lot of hugs, and there had been a few tears. But it was going to be wonderful to be there for her baby, to see him walk for the first time, to teach him herself instead of leaving it to a babysitter.

Bobby had gone with her and her mother to the piano recital over Father's Day weekend, and they'd had so much fun together with the baby. It had been a nice time away together, and Bobby was attentive to her and fussed over her mother as usual. That part never changed. There were times when Bobby wouldn't touch her, saying she was too fat. There were times when they argued or didn't speak to each other. But there was never a time when Bobby wasn't sweet and solicitous to Anna.

Bobby and Viki were planning to go to a fancy Dallas restaurant for their upcoming sixteenth wedding anniversary on July 5. Her mother was going to stay home with Monty. Viki was looking forward to an evening alone with her husband. Those were few, since he worked so much overtime at the police department with the tactical team. That anniversary weekend would be just for them.

———————

Cindy and Bobby worked cases together that next week. They worked out at the gym together. She was distant, and he was unhappy. They planned a trip to the range on Saturday. She'd had trouble qualifying the last time, and qualifications were looming again. He showed her some things she was doing wrong, and she improved her score.

He insisted she try shooting his Glock 9 mm pistol, which was identical to hers. But he had a new sight, he said, and he wanted to see if one like his helped her shooting. They agreed to practice again before qualifications, which were later in the year. He told her things were on track for him to move out on June 30.

Cindy remained suspicious. She went to the apartment complex where Bobby said he'd rented an apartment, and she used her badge to question the apartment manager. That was strictly against policy, but she had to know if Bobby was really leaving. She was performing a welfare check, she told the apartment manager. There had been some concern from family members that the man who rented the apartment might be suicidal because he was going through a divorce. The manager told her he knew Bobby, and yes, he had rented an apartment. The manager knew about the divorce and agreed to check. When he came back from using his key to the apartment, he said it was empty.

"No one has been inside there since we cleaned it for rental," he said. "The vacuum cleaner marks on the carpet haven't even been disturbed."

Cindy felt better. And then she felt guilty. How could she have not believed him? Would he go to the length and expense of renting an apartment if he didn't plan to move in? Still, he'd lied to her about his weekend trip. She was confused.

Bobby called her, upset. The apartment manager had called his home to let him know the apartment was ready, he said. And Viki had answered the telephone. He'd talked to the manager and told him not to call him at home again. That didn't make sense to Cindy. If Viki knew Bobby was moving out, she surely must know he had to have a place to live. The things Bobby said were not adding up.

June 30 arrived. Bobby's moving day. It was raining, and Cindy giggled to her friends that Bobby was going to get wet during his move. He didn't.

Instead, he called and asked where she was. She was on the interstate highway in Denton driving near the Radisson hotel. He told her to pull into the parking lot there and wait for him. Cindy did that, dreading what he would tell her next. She knew instinctively that Bobby was not moving that day. She didn't even want to know why. She just wanted to drive away. Her small boys were asleep in the backseat. She just wanted to go home and put them to bed. This didn't sound good.

They stayed in their cars, pulling them facing opposite directions so they could speak through their driver's windows. He handed her a white plastic container through the window. She looked at it, confused, and handed it back.

"What's this?"

Bobby read the label to her, but she still didn't know what it was or what it all meant.

"You know how I've been having bad headaches this past week? Well, I think this is the reason," he said dramatically. "I found this on the bar, and I think Viki's been putting it in my drinks. And Monty is sick. She's been giving him milk, and she knows he's allergic to milk."

"If you really think she's given you something poisonous, you need to go to the emergency room and have some tests run," Cindy said. "Why would she do this?"

"She told me she wanted to hurt me as badly as I've hurt her," he said. "We argued about it, and I slapped her. It's the first time I ever touched her physically, and she says if there is a mark she'll press charges."

Cindy's head was reeling. What on earth was this all about? Deep inside, though, she knew it was all about Bobby not leaving his wife.

"I can't leave Monty there with her. She's unstable. I don't know what she might do to him. You don't know what she's capable of."

He handed her a packet through the open car windows. It was all the letters and cards she had sent to him. He'd been keeping them in his desk at work, he said, but now he had to get them out of there. If there were an investigation into the slapping incident, his desk might be searched, and he couldn't let the other officers know he was having an affair. It would look bad for an assault charge.

"You need to just stay with your wife," she said. "I'm going to get on with my life." She gunned her car out of the parking lot.

Cindy lay awake all night with a stomachache. She didn't know what was true anymore and what was a lie. Had Bobby even filed for divorce? Had he really slapped Viki? How could all this be a lie when he began telling her about the divorce several months ago? Surely he wouldn't keep up a charade for that long!

She talked to her friend Jackie about it. Maybe he can't

leave but he doesn't want to lose you either, Jackie said. Cindy remembered a time when Bobby once jokingly told her that he'd use his gun if he caught her with another man. He said he'd rather be with her in eternity than see her with another man. "Accidents do happen," he said.

Cindy was suddenly scared. She called Jackie.

"If anything should happen to me or to Viki," she told her, "you'll know something is wrong. I'm getting afraid he might actually hurt one of us. I'm going to start taping my conversations with him."

Cindy was part of the Fourth of July parade through Denton that year. She was riding in a police car when her cell phone rang. It was Bobby. He wanted to wish her a good holiday, he said, and he wanted to ask her to give him a chance to make her believe in him again.

"I love you," he said. "Please don't give up on us. I'm going to find a way to make everything right again."

They didn't talk much at work on Friday, July 5. Cindy knew it was Bobby's wedding anniversary. She was cool, sitting across the aisle from him in the family services office. She said no to his invitation to lunch. Later, he asked for help serving a warrant, and she agreed. But instead, he drove to a restaurant. If she wasn't hungry she didn't have to eat, he said. But he wanted company while he had lunch. They ate and climbed back into his unmarked detective car.

"Can we go by your house for a little while?" he asked.

She knew that meant he wanted to have sex. On his sixteenth wedding anniversary with another woman. No, she said, they could not. He silently drove them back to the police department. Bobby was angry. Well, so was she.

He told her to have a good weekend when he left that afternoon. She didn't answer.

Cindy's cell phone rang sometime between 11 P.M. and midnight. She was sound asleep and had trouble getting focused. She grabbed a package of cigarettes and started out to the porch to smoke while she talked. Under stress in her relationship, she'd gone back to smoking. Bobby didn't know it and certainly would not approve. She stepped out on the porch and screamed, almost dropping her lighter. A man was standing there. After she caught her breath she realized that it was Bobby, calling from in front of her house.

"You scared me. What are you doing here?"

"I just wanted to kiss you," he said. "I knew you wouldn't want me to come over on my anniversary, so I waited till midnight. I just wanted to tell you that I am definitely moving. I know you don't trust me now, but I'm going to prove to you that I mean what I say and I can be trusted."

Tears welled up in her eyes. "I love you. I will always love you. But I don't have anything to believe in anymore."

"You can believe in me. I'm going to show you. I'm going to ride up on a white horse and take you away." He laughed. "Of course, the white horse will be a moving van."

They made love that night. After Bobby left, Cindy lay

awake thinking. She still didn't trust him. The lies had cut too deep. When he'd asked her to go shooting at the range with him the next day, a Saturday, she'd said no.

She and Jackie took their children to the lake the next morning. They stayed until about 3 P.M. Cindy's ex-husband was picking up the boys at 5 P.M., and then she had plans to go country dancing with some friends. She hadn't been out in a really long time. She thought her willingness to go meant she was finally breaking free of Bobby.

She took a short nap and got ready to go. She turned in front of the mirror. She was looking good in her tight-fitting jeans and boots. Maybe she'd meet a nice single guy. Her friends picked her up about 8:30 P.M. They stopped at an ATM so she could get cash, and then they went in the Rockin' Rodeo. Nothing much was going on there. They had a drink and decided to drive to a Dallas club. They had driven only a few miles when her cell phone rang. It was Jackie.

"Oh Cindy, you have to come home. Right now," her friend said.

No, nothing was wrong with the boys, but she wouldn't tell her why it was necessary to get home. Nevertheless, her friends turned around and drove back to Denton. Jackie met her at her house. She looked at Cindy with trepidation in her eyes.

"Cindy," she said, "Viki Lozano shot herself a couple of hours ago. She's dead. She's dead, Cindy!"

CHAPTER 7

MY WIFE HAS A GUNSHOT

On July 6, 2002, the 911 call came in at 9:05 P.M.

"I need an ambulance," came the male voice over the emergency line. "My wife has a gunshot."

The 911 operator elicited from the caller that he was police detective Bobby Lozano.

"Is she breathing?"

"I don't know. No. Hurry."

The dispatcher asked Bobby to check to see if she was breathing. He was gone for a few seconds and then came back to the telephone. She was not. He said he'd come home and found her slumped over in the bed with his Glock 9 mm service pistol beside her. The dispatcher asked if he would begin CPR. He said he would and laid down the telephone. Twenty-five seconds later he was back, asking where the ambulance was.

The ambulance was nearly there, along with a fire engine, per protocol. It wasn't the equipment that was needed on the fire engine; it was the manpower. Engine Six and Medic Six came from the nearby Station Six and were on the scene in four minutes.

Six firefighter/paramedics ran to the house. They had been told by a dispatcher en route that they were heading to a victim with a gunshot wound who was not conscious and not breathing. CPR was in progress, the dispatcher said.

A man was waiting for them at the front door, holding a baby.

"Where are they?" paramedic Brandon Galbraith asked the man, referring to the victim and whoever was performing CPR. The man pointed, and the crew rushed into a large bedroom area and stopped short. There was no one performing CPR. A woman was lying on the bed with a large bloodstain under her left side. They could see from the door that lividity had set in. Blood was pooled, blanching the foot and leg halfway up the calf in one of her legs, which was dangling off the bed. Galbraith felt for a pulse. There was none. He pulled back the rubber glove from the back of his hand and felt her skin. It was cold. *This woman has been dead a long time, and no CPR has been performed*, he thought. Dispatchers routinely told callers to pull a patient off of a bed and onto the floor for a hard surface to start CPR. She had not been moved. Galbraith gently lifted the woman's shoulder and pulled aside the back of her pajama top. Her back also showed evidence of lividity.

The man knelt near the bed, crying, with the baby in his

arms. Galbraith saw the baby looking down at the woman. Realizing that this was most likely the infant's mother, Galbraith took the child and left the room with him. But the baby began to cry. He heard another paramedic tell the man to leave the room, and he came out and took the crying baby back from Galbraith.

Paramedic Brad Imel spoke to the man, who said he had been planning to clean his gun, but then had to leave the house for a short time. "I told her to leave the gun alone," he said. But when he returned, he found her with the gunshot wound.

The other paramedics began gathering their medical equipment. There was nothing they could do here.

———————

Denton police officer Dale Binkert was the first officer on the scene. When he arrived, firefighters were straightening their medical bags and carrying the empty stretcher back out to the ambulance. Binkert didn't recognize Bobby Lozano. The veteran officer was working a possible crime scene and not thinking the man with the baby might be someone he knew. Binkert walked into the bedroom and stood at the foot of the bed. He saw what appeared to be a gun-cleaning kit lying beside the victim and a Glock pistol near her left hand. He walked out of the room and radioed dispatch to notify the on-call detective and police social worker Richard Godoy.

Then Binkert told the homeowner he would need to complete a statement. When the man continued walking away, he called sharply out to him. The man turned.

"It's Detective Lozano," he said. "That's my wife in there."

"I'm really sorry, Bobby. I didn't recognize you at first. I wouldn't have yelled at you like that. I'm really sorry for your loss."

Officer Rachel Key arrived next. Binkert stationed her near the bedroom door and asked her to log anyone entering the room in and out on a log sheet. She saw two dogs through the bedroom door. She walked into the room and looked at the woman on the bed. She asked Sergeant Lee Creamer, who had just arrived, to shut the dogs away, and then Key left the room and remained outside the bedroom door until the early morning hours, carefully noting who entered and who left and at what times. She heard Bobby talking to different people as they arrived, especially his relatives, who gathered in the living area. He'd been about to clean his gun when he decided to go to the tanning salon first, he told his mother-in-law. He told Viki not to touch the gun, but she apparently decided to clean it for him.

"You know she was always taking things into her own hands and doing things for other people," he said.

About 3:15 A.M. all the on-scene investigations were finished and the crime scene team was leaving. Officer Key drove back to the police department and wrote a brief report, consisting mostly of the log of officers in and out of the room. But Key also wrote that both Viki Lozano's legs were hanging off the bed, and that lividity was present in both legs. All the other reports only noted that one of

Viki's legs had been hanging off the bed. This discrepancy would later cause trouble at the trial.

Later Key would say that she'd been tired and didn't remember the scene correctly when she wrote the report.

———————

Detective Lieutenant Lee Howell lived in the country outside Denton. He'd just returned from dinner in town that Saturday night when his pager vibrated at about 9:20 P.M. He called dispatch to find out what was going on. Bobby Lozano's wife was dead, he learned. Gunshot wound in the chest. Howell knew his Saturday night off had suddenly become a work night. He changed clothing and headed back into town.

Once at the house on Denton's south side, he found Detective Jeff Wawro and Patrol Sergeant Lee Creamer waiting for him. The scene had been secured, he learned. An officer stood at the door to the bedroom, actually a suite that took up the whole north wing of the house. The entrance to the room faced an alcove that held an office with a computer and other items of office equipment. Next to that, across from the bed, was a kitchenette area with cabinets, a sink, a microwave oven and a small refrigerator. Just to the right of the door was a playpen. And farther to the right lay the king-sized bed. It was a canopy bed, and the top was laced with bright silk scarves of varying colors. Nightstands sat on either side of the bed, and a large-screen television hung on the wall opposite. A small sitting area with a couch and chair took up the end of the room under a window facing the street. A hallway near the television on the south wall led to a "wardrobe room," two other closets (one of them cedar-lined), a laundry room and a large bathroom with a big, round black marble spa tub. There was also a shower and a sauna area in the bathroom.

Howell took control of the situation. He radioed dispatch and asked that members of the crime scene team be contacted and sent to the La Mancha Lane house. He called Sergeant Steve Macsas and left a message on his voice mail. He greeted Detective Benny Parkey as he arrived. He and Parkey agreed that Parkey would not be part of the investigative team. Parkey and Bobby had been partners and friends, and Howell wanted him to be available for the family. Bobby stayed away from Howell and from Parkey, however, and as the evening progressed, from all the officers on the scene.

Howell talked it over with Lieutenant Lonnie Flemming, the other ranking officer at the house, and they decided it would be best to call in the Texas Rangers to head the investigation since it involved one of their own detectives. Howell spoke to Ranger Tracy Murphree by telephone, and Murphree said he was out of town but would get there as quickly as he could. Sergeant Macsas also called and promised to respond. Howell was gathering his team. He didn't suspect then that the shooting was anything more than Bobby Lozano said it was: a terrible accident. Still, there was a procedure for handling a shooting death, and it would be followed. Howell did, however, tell the other officers to show as much respect for the family as possible and allow them to stay in the other part of the house. Later he would wish he hadn't.

This was quite a large group to be smack in the middle of a crime scene. This was not protocol. The police should have asked everyone to leave the house. They should have gone through every room looking for clues to the death in the master bedroom. But the officers considered only the bedroom off-limits at this point, and the family was far away from the bedroom in the huge house.

They had no idea that day, or for weeks afterward, that they should have been looking for a bag or a bowl of popcorn. They didn't know there was popcorn in Viki's stomach, in her mouth, under her loose pajama top—which meant that she must've been eating the popcorn in bed; but none was visible anywhere in the bedroom.

They should have been more suspicious. But this was the wife of a fellow law enforcement officer. He said her death was a gun-cleaning accident. The kit was there on the bed. If not an accident, they thought, then maybe suicide. They felt sorry for him. They didn't want to cause this family more misery than they had to. It was a bad situation, and they considered Bobby a good officer who needed their help.

―――――

Police social worker Richard Godoy was next to arrive at the big house on the corner in the well-to-do neighborhood of Montecito Del Sur. He'd been there several times before. He and Bobby were good friends. Now it was his job to help Bobby and his family. He went to Bobby after greeting officers Key and Binkert. Bobby was in the kitchen, looking lost, holding his eleven-month-old son, Monty.

"What happened?" Godoy asked.

"I went to tan and when I got home she was on the bed with my gun," he said. "I couldn't have been gone more than thirty minutes. I called out to her when I came in the house and she didn't answer. I went into the bedroom, and she was in there on the bed. I tried to do CPR, but I couldn't get her to breathe."

Godoy looked at Bobby carefully. He was a social worker, but he had been to the police academy. He was present at most crime scenes that involved death. He knew the ropes. There was no blood in evidence anywhere on Bobby. How could he have performed CPR on a chest wound and not be covered in blood?

"What was Viki doing with your gun?"

"We were going to the range tomorrow to shoot and I needed to clean it. I laid it out on the bed to clean before I left."

Godoy watched his friend. He was grimacing as he spoke as though he were crying. But no tears fell from his eyes. Godoy found a Coke for Bobby and poured it into a glass for him.

Bobby hadn't called any family members. His mother-in-law, Anna Farish, was teaching piano late in Plano and wouldn't be home until around 11 P.M., he said. He asked Godoy to contact her pastor so he could be there when Anna arrived. Godoy began calling Bobby's brothers and his parents, not telling them that Viki was dead but saying there had been a tragedy and they needed to come over. He couldn't reach Bobby's sister, Blanca, at either of her telephone numbers, so he left messages on both for her to come to the house.

Bobby didn't seem to have a number for Viki's brother, David Farish, so Godoy called the airlines where he worked as a pilot and explained the situation. He left his telephone number and asked them to call David and give him the number.

Frank Lozano, Bobby's brother, arrived and broke into tears when he heard the news, as did Frank's wife, Tricia. But she went to the baby, who was then sleeping in a playpen in his room on the opposite side of the house.

Javier Lozano drove up, and Godoy greeted him. Godoy worked out at Javier's small gym and knew him well. Javier was shocked. He paced the porch saying, "This can't be happening." Finally, he went in to comfort Bobby and then sat by himself, away from the family, for the rest of the night.

The elder Lozanos arrived and joined the group in the huge living and kitchen area in the back of the house.

David Farish arrived and hurried into the house. Frank decided to go to pick up Blanca, who still had not returned Godoy's telephone messages. He returned with her shortly afterward. There must be some mistake, she said as she exited the car.

"Where are the paramedics?" Blanca demanded. "What's going on here?"

Godoy explained that the paramedics had come and gone. There had been nothing they could do.

———————

Texas Ranger Tracy Murphree was at a concert at Bass Hall in Fort Worth. Robert Earl Keen sang his popular redneck Christmas song, "Merry Christmas from the Family."

"Mom got drunk and Dad got drunk at our Christmas party," he crooned. "Merry Christmas from the family. Feliz Navidad."

Murphree laughed along with his fiancée and thousands of other Keen fans. Then he felt his cell phone vibrate. He looked at the display. Lee Howell. If Lee was calling him on a Saturday night, something bad had happened. Damn! The tickets weren't cheap, and his fiancée was going to be disappointed. But Murphree knew they weren't going to be watching the rest of the concert. They were heading back to Denton. He walked out into the lobby to take the call, and Howell explained the situation. Denton police needed his help, and Murphree was on his way.

Rangers were investigators. Helping local law enforcement officers with his expertise, adding state resources to sometimes meager city resources, was a major part of the job. Providing a layer of distance from an investigation involving another law enforcement officer was just a smart move.

Driving back, Murphree thought about what he had learned and considered what he knew about Detective Bobby Lozano. The crude term "pussy hound" came to mind. There had been rumors that Lozano was having an affair with Officer Cindy Waters. Could this have a bearing on this shooting? Probably not, Murphree thought. From what he had heard, Lozano had carried on dozens of affairs. Why would this one be different?

———

Detectives Jeff Wawro (who would be lead on the case), Craig Fitzgearld, Jason Grellhesl and Russell Lewis all entered the bedroom at 10:56 P.M. Wawro and Lewis began photographing the scene while the others made a cursory search around the bed. No one touched the bed at this point.

Lieutenant Lee Howell stayed outside to wait for Ranger Murphree and Sergeant Steve Macsas. He saw Viki Lozano's mother, Anna Farish, pull into the driveway. He walked to her car door, and she rolled down the window. "What is happening?" Anna asked. "What are all these people doing at my home?"

"Ma'am, I'm Lee Howell. I need for you to come out of the car, and we'll go inside the house and talk." Bobby had asked that he be the one to tell Viki's mother that her daughter was dead.

"I'm not getting out of this car until you tell me what's happening," she said, a high, hysterical note creeping into her voice. "You tell me right now."

Richard Godoy had been waiting for Anna, and he walked out to the car. Howell stepped back and allowed Godoy to coax Anna into the house.

"I'm so sorry!" Bobby burst out when he saw her. "This wasn't supposed to happen."

He held his hysterical mother-in-law as she wailed over and over, "Not my Viki! Why is God doing this to me?"

Godoy heard Bobby repeat the story of the gun cleaning and the tanning salon. Mrs. Farish began to heave, as though she were going to throw up. Godoy found a bowl in case that happened and led her to a chair. Bobby sat next to her, and Blanca sat close to her brother. Then the pastor took charge and they all began to pray.

———

Ranger Tracy Murphree and Sergeant Steve Macsas arrived about the same time at the house on La Mancha, and Howell briefed them. He had waited to go inside, leaving preliminary investigations to his team. Nothing could be moved anyway until the medical examiner investigator showed up.

There was little traffic on the streets of the exclusive neighborhood, but Howell noticed that when cars passed, they slowed as drivers tried to figure out what was happening. The three officers went into the house and into the bedroom suite. Viki was lying on the right side of the bed, her head near but not touching the pillow. It was cocked slightly to the left but facing upward. Her eyes were half open. Her right leg was hanging off the bed, and her left leg appeared to be bent at the knee. It was covered by the bedclothes. Her right hand was hanging off the bed. She was wearing blue pajamas with a yellow duck pattern on them. In the center of her chest Howell could see a small round hole in the pajamas with blood around it. He could see that the mattress and sheet under her left side were soaked in blood, and he could see small amounts of blood on her right hand.

Her left hand was flung out by her left side. Near it lay a Glock 9 mm pistol on top of a single sheet of newspaper, part of the classified section of that day's *Denton Record-Chronicle*. There was a small beige towel also on the newspaper. Howell also saw a brown box that appeared to be a gun-cleaning kit with various tools inside. A can of Break Free gun oil was lying on its side near the box. Oddly, a pair of dirty white socks that appeared to have come from a laundry basket were lying on one side of the box. Howell thought the socks looked as if they had been dropped on the box from above. There was a large oil stain on the newspaper, and the Glock looked like it had been sprayed down from one end to the other with oil. Every area of the gun was dripping oil, from the slide to the bottom of the grips. Another oddity, since Bobby undoubtedly knew you only needed a couple of drops of oil on the metal workings inside the Glock.

Howell asked Detective Russell Lewis, his crime scene recorder, if he had brought the alternate light source. It essentially was a black light that would show up minute particles of blood or semen or other evidence that was not immediately apparent in regular light. Blood looked black under the light. Semen fluoresced. If sexual assault were a factor, the light was handy. Lewis said he hadn't brought the light, and Howell sent him back to the police department to fetch it.

Howell then left the bedroom to his handpicked crime scene team and walked outside. Frank Lozano, Bobby's brother, came up to him. Frank was also a longtime police officer, with the University of North Texas.

"Is Bobby going to be a suspect in anything?" he wanted to know.

"At this point I have no reason to suspect him of anything," Howell said. "But we have to treat this case as any other and do what we have to do."

"I understand," Frank said, and he went back to the family.

Wawro directed the crime scene search. No one touched the bed, because the medical examiner investigator had not arrived yet and everything had to be preserved just as it was until he had finished his own investigation. Detectives Fitzgearld and Grellhesl searched the rest of the bedroom. They both had nice homes, but nothing like this luxurious suite.

The detectives didn't touch the bed, but they looked hard on it for the shell casing from the Glock. It would have kicked out the right side when the bullet was fired. They couldn't see the casing on the bed or on the floor. They looked behind the draperies, under a chair. They ran their hands through the pristine carpet. Grellhesl crawled under the bed. No shell casing.

Fitzgearld helped Grellhesl search the office area, looking in each drawer and cabinet of the desk. They found some cards from Viki to Bobby telling him how much she loved him and their baby son. A wastebasket held only a receipt from a Lewisville Target store dated earlier that day. Grellhesl noticed that a game of some sort was on pause on the computer.

Finally, Dwight Crawford, the medical examiner investigator, arrived, explaining that he was so late because he'd been on the south side of the county working a fatal accident. Only one investigator was on call at a time at night in the small Denton County investigator's office that was overseen by contract with the Tarrant County Medical Examiner's Office. Crawford began to examine the body. He found the spent bullet that had exited Viki's side low under her arm inside her pajamas. It had not penetrated the back of her pajama top. They put the mangled bullet in a film container, and Grellhesl poked airholes in the lid with his knife so the blood would dry.

Crawford bagged Viki's hands in brown paper bags so no evidence would be lost. If there had been a struggle, there might be DNA under her fingernails. Later, the district attorney would claim that Crawford had bungled a gunshot residue test on Viki's hands. Crawford angrily responded that he hadn't done a gunshot residue test in the field. His job was to make sure the evidence was preserved for the autopsy, and he did that. Regardless of how that test was performed, however, ultimately it could not be used in court because the swab that was supposed to be clean to show the test began with a clean set of swabs had been contaminated. The officials agreed, though, that whether Viki had handled the gun herself or just held her hands up in defensive mode, the residue would have been all over her hands because of the almost point-blank range at which the gun was fired.

Crawford allowed the funeral home attendants to lift Viki to a gurney for the trip to the medical examiner's office for autopsy. Blood gushed out of her side and stained the beige carpet when they moved her. Before that, all the carpet had shown was fresh steam cleaner grooves. Bobby told the investigators later that he had cleaned the carpet that afternoon while his wife did some laundry.

With Viki's body gone, the detectives could begin their real investigation. They had photographed the scene from every angle with her body still on the bed. Now they carefully lifted each piece of evidence from its place on the bed, photographing it before and after they moved it, and Lewis logged it onto the report. They first moved everything to the foot of the bed, another small mistake that would later hurt their case. They should have put everything into evidence bags as soon as items were moved, and logged items in the order they removed them. Wawro picked up the gun and cleared it, dropping the magazine. It was fully loaded except for the round that went through Viki Lozano. With latex gloves on their hands, the officers examined the gun oilcan. They saw what appeared to be a smeared bloody fingerprint on the bottom of the can. Someone, not Viki, had touched her blood and then touched the can. She would not have been moving anything after that bullet tore through her. They moved the cleaning kit. They moved the oil-stained newspaper. The blanket was furled into wrinkles under the newspaper, and there were bloodstains on it. How could blood have gotten *under* the newspaper without staining it?

Wawro began carefully spreading the wrinkles in the blanket with his fingers. And inside one of the folds lay the shell casing.

They carefully removed the bloody bedding, folded it and placed it into garbage bags. It was July, summer in Texas. But on top of the sheets they found a comforter, an electric blanket and a colorful blanket with a tiger design. Someone in the house was cold natured, it seemed. Or they kept the air-conditioning so cold that they had to cover up at night. Everything was bundled up for a trip to the medical examiner's office.

Nowhere in the bedroom did they find evidence of a popcorn bowl. But at the time, they didn't know that popcorn would become important in the case. They didn't know there was popcorn under Viki's loose pajamas and even a small piece in her mouth. Viki could not have moved the container herself without losing the kernels that were still under her loose pajamas. But if Viki didn't carry the popcorn bowl out of the bedroom, who did? These questions would only come to them later.

Grellhesl and Fitzgearld, on Howell's orders, walked through the rest of the house looking for anything that seemed out of place. There was a bucket of pinkish water near the front door, which Bobby said was water he used earlier in the day to clean the door. Everything else was tidy, clean and apparently undisturbed. They made routine checks of Anna's suite and the baby's room. They opened closet doors in the numerous other rooms and checked for blood spots. But out of respect for a fellow officer, they didn't go through drawers or poke behind clothes in the closets. The search was superficial. They walked around the outside of the house. There was no sign of forced entry. All the detectives left the house about 3:15 A.M.

Bobby began to talk to Richard Godoy, who was not only there as the police social worker, whose job it was to try to help family members in any way he could, but as a friend. Bobby said he kept thinking of when he was a member of the tactical team that went after a man who had kidnapped his small son on the Texas Woman's University campus and held him hostage in the top of a tall tower building. The man eventually released the little boy and shot himself in the head. Bobby had watched the man bleed and die. It had "fucked me up," he now said. He acknowledged that he should have talked to Godoy back then, but he hadn't wanted to appear weak, he said. Bobby also talked about the night his squad car, running Code Four (fast and with his police lights off), had been en route to a burglary in progress. A car pulled out in front of him, and he struck it, killing a baby inside. He'd been unable to let the dead baby out of his arms, he said, and the other officers had had to pry the baby away from him.

"Why am I thinking of these things now?" he asked Godoy.

Godoy explained how cumulative stress could affect emergency personnel until one day, a traumatic situation acted as a trigger and brought back all the repressed feelings from all those other times. Bobby nodded. He still wasn't crying any actual tears, even when he sobbed and his shoulders shook, Godoy noticed.

"Why is this taking so long?" Bobby then asked.

He should know, Godoy thought. Bobby had done crime scene investigations himself numerous times. He knew exactly what the police were doing and why it took them so long.

What about funeral arrangements? Bobby wanted to know. Godoy said he had a packet of information that would help him with all that.

"How do I go about getting her cremated? She has always said she wanted cremation. Who does that around here?"

My God, Godoy thought. His wife was still lying in their bed, still in their house, and Bobby was inquiring about how to have her cremated?

"Viki's with her father now," Bobby said. Viki's father had died in 1995, several years earlier.

"It's OK," Blanca said. "We only get one shot at life, and you have to make it count."

Godoy flinched. Poor choice of words. But what in the world did she mean by that anyway?

———

The police officers on the scene watched the family but did not interact with them. They did not interview Bobby that night. The officers there had never dealt with such a circumstance. They were uneasy; they knew something was off, but they didn't give their police instincts credence that night. This was the home of one of their own. A brother in their tight law enforcement family. They were a little lax on protocol because of that. They allowed the family to stay in the living area of the huge house. They looked in closets and drawers all over the house, but they limited their detailed investigation to the bedroom suite.

Later, they would regret that.

———

Lieutenant Lee Howell had stayed mostly out of the bedroom, allowing his crime scene team, headed by Jeff Wawro, to do its work. Sergeant Steve Macsas had also remained largely outside. Both of them later wished they had taken command of the scene.

Murphree recalled that he had been in the "poor Bobby" mode when he helped with the crime scene. He was a young Ranger, with only a few murder investigations under his belt. In his job, mostly you learned by doing, he said. You make mistakes. You learn from them. You don't make those mistakes again.

"The idea that Bobby did it was the farthest thing from my mind that night. You don't want to think that another officer would do a thing like that. We should never have allowed all those people to stay in the house, but we did," Murphree said. "I've never done that again, and I never will."

So some things that might have been done were not done. Not as a measure to cover anything up, but because too much trust was put in a fellow officer. No one searched

Bobby's car. No one drove the route from the house to the tanning salon, checking Dumpsters along the way for possible discarded evidence. They did not check Bobby's hands for gunshot residue, and they did not take a statement from him that night.

All those things would haunt them later.

CHAPTER 8

THE AFTERMATH

Lieutenant Lee Howell met Monday morning, July 8, 2002, with Rangers Tony Bennie and Tracy Murphree. Murphree said that since he had worked closely with all the Denton detectives, he thought it would be proper to bring another Ranger into the case to ensure there was no misconception of impropriety. Howell agreed, and the three officers went over the evidence they had gathered at the scene. And they discussed the problem of the rumored affair Detective Bobby Lozano had been carrying on with Officer Cindy Waters.

Cindy hadn't been able to sleep that Saturday night. She'd lain awake, wondering what really had happened. Had

Viki found out about her and Bobby and shot herself? It seemed the most likely scenario. Cindy cried at the thought that her affair might have driven a woman to suicide. A woman with a baby. And what about Bobby? How must he be feeling? If Cindy had done this, she thought, if she had not done that, if Bobby hadn't been planning to move out, would Viki still be alive?

On Monday morning Cindy began looking for her supervisor, Sergeant Roger White, but she couldn't find him. Lieutenant Lonnie Flemming wasn't in his office either. She had a burden she needed to dump. She feared what would happen when people found out about the affair, but she knew for certain that she had to tell them before they found out on their own. She discovered Lee Howell in his office. She had to talk to him immediately, she said. He called Flemming to join them, and Cindy just started talking. She talked and she cried and she paused to compose herself and then she burst into another flurry of words. When she was empty and weeping, they asked her if she had talked to Bobby since Saturday. She had not, she said. If she spoke to him, she must tell them immediately what was said, Howell told her, and she agreed. Go home, he said. Get some rest. You'll be on leave for a while.

Cindy also showed Howell a card that Bobby had given her, filled with words of love. Were there other cards? he asked. Cindy said she had numerous cards and letters from Bobby, and that he'd recently given her back the ones she had given him. She told Howell about the conversation she and Bobby had through their car windows about a possible investigation into Bobby slapping Viki and how he told her he had to give her back the mementos that he kept in his desk so they wouldn't be found.

Howell followed her home, and she handed over all the letters, pulling them down from a Victoria's Secret shopping bag on a closet shelf.

She checked her voice mail after Howell left. There was a message from Bobby she apparently had received the night before. *I know you know what happened by now*, the message said. *I know tomorrow will be a hard day for you. Keep your chin up*.

Tuesday night Bobby finally called her.

"Are you OK?" he asked.

"No, no I'm not. . . . I'm so sorry about Viki," she said. "How are you?"

"I'm with my family. The hardest part is that every time someone walks into the room Monty looks up to see if it is his mother. . . . Um, my days are running together here. Was it Thursday or Friday when I came over to your house?"

It was Friday, she told him.

"You just need to tell them the truth," she said. "Just tell them everything."

"I did. Uh, did you tell them about the 'D'?"

Cindy understood that he meant the divorce. He was not alone in the house.

"I told them everything," she said. "I have to tell them anytime we talk and what was said. Bobby, I know you are not involved in this. But I don't even know what happened!"

"At this point, it's better that you don't know. Right

now, I'm just trying to get through tomorrow. Listen, there are a lot of people here and I can't talk. I don't know when I'll be able to call you again."

Unable to go to work, shut out from the investigation, Cindy worried and cried and chastised herself for her part in what must have been a suicide. Cindy was a woman with a big heart. She was a mother. She suffered over little Monty, now motherless. She suffered over her part in whatever had happened to Viki Lozano. She worried about her job. What would she do if she lost it? She loved being a police detective. If she was fired from the Denton department, would another police department hire her? How would she support her own two baby boys?

The questions were always there, swirling around in her head, keeping her from sleep.

Cindy didn't hear from Bobby for weeks after that. What was happening? Would she lose her job? Would Bobby? What about that wonderful dream they had planned together? Viki had been cremated, she learned. She feared that ashes were all that were left of her life as well.

When Howell returned to the police department Monday afternoon after retrieving the letters from Cindy Waters, Detective Bryan Lee asked to talk to him. Cindy's desk calendars contained a lot of notations, he said. He thought some of them might refer to Bobby. Howell collected the calendars and asked a computer tech to take the computers from Bobby's and Cindy's desks and check for any correspondence between them.

That evening, Bobby drove to the office on Loop 288 to meet with Rangers Tracy Murphree and Tony Bennie, and with Detective Mike Bateman, who was a friend of Bobby's and who thought he might be able to help.

By the time the interview was over, however, Bateman would come to the conclusion that his friend was a murderer.

Murphree was a staunch Dallas Cowboys fan, a passionate patriot and a devout Texan to the core. Over his right shoulder, as he sat behind his desk, was a large picture of the late, great Cowboys coach Tom Landry. Over his left shoulder hung a drawing of another of his heroes, Ronald Reagan.

They gathered in the Ranger's office. Bobby said he would like to type his own statement, and Murphree moved from his desk chair and let Bobby work on his computer. It took hours. The officers left him to it and sat in another office to give him privacy while he typed. When it was done, Bobby printed it and signed it, and they asked him some questions.

Show us how Viki was on the bed when you walked into the room, they asked. Bobby leaned over in his chair to the left of his knees, as far over as he could. "*She was sitting up about like this*," he said.

No way, the Ranger thought.

They sent Bobby to sit in another area of the state law enforcement office where Murphree's office was situated. Then they settled in to read the statement. First one Ranger then the other stared at the pages, muttering and shaking his head. When they finished, they began going over it again. Never in either of their careers had they seen such an odd statement. They were stunned.

Bobby Lozano's statement about the death of his wife began with a detailed description of their anniversary dinner, the day before Viki's death:

On the evening of July 5th, 2002, my wife and I had gone out to celebrate our sixteenth wedding anniversary. I had made dinner reservations for the restaurant named "Il Sole" near Highland Park in Dallas. The reservations were for 9 p.m. We arrived on time and we were seated for dinner. I recall that we decided to eat from the three-course meal "chef's special." This particular dinner is accompanied by a special wine for each of the three phases of dinner (the appetizer, main course and dessert). I recall that my wife and I spent the entire dinner reminiscing about how fortunate we were to have born a child so beautiful as my son, Monty. We spoke of his growth from birth to present day. We also spoke of his future and how excited we were that she would have the opportunity to be with him at home over the course of the next year.

Viki had decided to take a year off from teaching school to spend quality time with the baby. She didn't want her son raised by a babysitter, Bobby wrote, and he agreed that would be the best course for their baby. If all went well, he said later, she even hoped to stay home until Monty turned five or six.

They returned home from their anniversary dinner

about 11:30 P.M., he wrote in the statement to police. They were surprised to see that Monty was wide awake when they walked in and was playing with Anna in the "great room."

Once Monty saw us, he giggled ever so mischievously as if to make sure that we knew that [he knew] we had left the house after he went to sleep earlier that night.

In a confusing segue, Bobby then began recalling a night back in April when he had made plans for just the two of them to go out and celebrate Viki's birthday, but that when they heard Monty crying as they left, they'd both looked at each other and knew that they couldn't possibly have a good time knowing their son was sad at home. They went back inside and were content to spend her birthday evening playing with Monty and eating leftovers.

Bobby then resumed talking about the anniversary night, how they'd stayed up for a while to play with the baby before going to sleep, then all got up early the next morning and went to the park, since Monty had been a little under the weather. The statement went on to describe in detail a fever the baby had had the previous week, and how they'd taken him to a pediatrician who ran numerous tests, including chest X-rays, stool samples and blood tests, but could find nothing wrong and eventually said that perhaps he was just teething.

(All this, and Bobby had not yet gotten to the purpose of his statement. He was supposed to be writing about his wife's death, yet he was talking about stool samples.)

One particular memory which remains close to my heart was having watched Viki swing Monty while he wrapped his arms around her neck. He was face down on her chest as she quietly sang a lullaby to him. I remember thinking how peaceful and secure he felt within his mother's embrace as he drifted off to sleep while they swung. I made a comment about how beautiful the moment appeared and the look on her face, which defined utter happiness and appreciation for Monty's life.

After arriving back at the house, Bobby wrote, the three of them took a bath together. Viki had rust on her hands from the chain on the swing, he recalled, and they were all sweaty from having played on the wooden structure at the park.

According to the statement, while Monty then took a nap, the couple did housework: Viki did laundry, and Bobby decided to steam clean the bedroom carpet. (This was important to his story, since the carpet around the bed still contained fresh steamer tracks when police arrived hours later.) After the baby awoke, the three of them again went out, this time to run errands at a Super Target. Bobby said that as they stood in the checkout line, he saw that Viki had quietly also picked up two more toys for Monty. When she saw that he had noticed the toys, they both laughed out loud. Viki bought numerous educational toys for the baby, who was quite spoiled when it came to toys, Bobby wrote.

They returned home about 4:30 P.M. and had dinner in

the kitchen, then once again bathed the baby and played with him until about 7 P.M., when he fell asleep in his crib. The doctor called about that time to inquire about Monty's condition. Bobby said he spoke to the doctor and told him that Viki was worried the baby's stool might contain blood. The doctor suggested that they not be overly concerned, but to schedule another appointment if things seemed the same the next day. Bobby wrote that he thanked the doctor for his concern, and for calling on a weekend to check on the baby.

(Bobby apparently felt that details of his son's minor illness were relevant to his wife's death somehow. Or was he simply padding a statement that got much less detailed the closer he got to the time of his wife's death?)

Bobby then went on to explain how he started playing a computer game that involved removing puzzle pieces in a certain order. Viki was on the bed watching TV. His wife was not feeling well, he now revealed. For about a week, he said, she had suffered from what she believed to be anemia. She was listless and extremely tired, and she lay there while he played the computer game in the office alcove of their bedroom suite.

Then he decided to clean his gun, he wrote. They had made plans to visit the gun range the next day, and he wanted to "take a moment" to clean his service weapon, a Glock 9 mm pistol. He had been to the range the prior weekend and had ammunition left over, he explained, so he wanted to shoot again. Viki had decided that it would be fine to take the baby along to the shooting range. If

Monty were "adversely affected" by the loud noise, they would simply return home.

Bobby wrote that he unfolded a section of that day's newspaper ("I don't recall what section it was," he noted) and laid it on his side of the bed, then placed his gun-cleaning box on the newspaper and took his Glock from the shoulder holster. He removed the fully loaded magazine from the pistol and ejected the round from the chamber. He left it with the slide locked open.

At this point, however, Bobby decided to stop what he was doing and leave to go to the tanning salon in the middle of the cleaning process. (Despite the fact that Bobby was Hispanic and had naturally brown skin, he complained to his coworkers at the police department that the color wasn't even. So he often lay in the tanning bed to keep his skin an even color.) He said he asked Viki *"if she didn't mind that after I cleaned the gun if I could go to tan. She offered to clean my gun while I went to tan so that we would have a little more time together when I returned. I told her not to worry about it since it would take only a few moments to clean the gun. As I started to take the rags from the cleaning box, I changed my mind and decided to go and tan first and then return to clean the gun. I didn't want to leave the residue of the cleaning fluids on my hands when I went to tan. She again offered to do it for me and I told her to relax. . . . I bent over and I kissed her forehead and said that I would be right back."*

He tanned for twenty minutes and then had a conversation with the desk clerk about what he did over the recent

Fourth of July holiday. (Police later surmised that Bobby was making sure the clerk would remember he'd been there. The clerk testified that Bobby had never once before said a word to him.)

He wrote that he arrived back at the house about 9 P.M.

I noticed that Viki was lying somewhat awkwardly on the bed. She was facedown and slightly to the left of her left hip. I asked her if she was feeling ill and I received no response. As I continued to walk around to her side of the bed, I again asked her if she was okay. I then noticed the newspaper and the cleaning box had been moved from where I left it. I think I may have again asked if she was okay but this time it was much more frantically. I raised her up and as if it were in slow motion, her listless body fell backward onto the pillow nearest the metal headboard. I saw her tongue hanging out of her mouth and the color of her face was extremely pale. I looked down where she had laid and I noticed a lot of blood on the sheets. I grabbed her by the shoulder and I screamed for her to respond. She remained completely lifeless as I repeatedly shook her to have her regain consciousness. When I saw the hole in the middle chest portion of her nightgown I knew that she had been shot. I then thought only to run to the bedroom telephone to call 911. I don't remember which dispatcher answered but I know that I might have been completely unintelligible as I screamed for an ambulance.

Bobby wrote that at this point, he suddenly thought about Monty. (His live-in mother-in-law, Anna, was gone for the evening.) He ran across the house to the baby's bedroom and snatched him up, startling the baby out of a sound sleep.

I ran back to the telephone in the bedroom and I again spoke with the dispatcher. . . . She asked that I begin CPR until the paramedics arrived. I think that I placed Monty down on the floor near the telephone as I ran back to Viki's side of the bed. . . . Although I did not straddle her body, I did begin CPR procedures from her side of the bed. I know that I was failing to do it properly because I was overcome with emotion. I begged her not to die and not to leave us alone. Moments later, I think, I ran back to the phone to tell the dispatcher that she was either not breathing or that she was unconscious (perhaps neither or both).

He picked up the baby and ran to the front door, he wrote. He opened it and turned on several outside lights. He wasn't sure what happened after that. He couldn't remember if he spoke to the dispatcher again. Bobby said that he ran out to meet the paramedics when they arrived and led them into the bedroom.

I vividly recall one of the ambulance personnel to have lifted my wife's top to verify where the gunshot was located. He looked down toward her right leg and foot which hung over the side of the bed onto the floor. I'm not sure what he saw or what he was thinking but he seemed quite taken aback. In ultimate desperation I asked him or them why they weren't working to revive her. He solemnly looked at me and said that there was nothing that he could do for her. I was in utter disbelief. I believe that I walked out of the bedroom and into the foyer and fell to one knee. As I continued to cry more and more, Monty became more and more upset to the point that he too began crying intensely. I recall one of the paramedics asking if he could take him from me for a moment. I was not going to allow him to be taken from my arms as I clutched him closely to my chest. From here, it seemed an eternity as uniformed police began to arrive.

Bobby recalled Officer Binkert offering him condolences but also telling him that he needed a statement about what had happened to his wife. Bobby said he looked at the officer in disbelief and turned his back on him, as Binkert yelled at him to come back. He made it clear that he held no hard feelings against Officer Binkert, however, who he said apologized for not recognizing Bobby, and who later "pulled me into his chest and allowed me to simply cry. It was all that I could do," Bobby wrote.

According to the statement to police that Bobby wrote, the medical examiner didn't arrive for hours. The crime scene team arrived and worked for a long time in the bedroom with the door shut. When the attendants came to take Viki away, already wrapped in a body bag, he asked to see her one last time. They agreed, as long as he didn't touch her.

When her face was revealed I promised to always raise Monty how she would have wanted me to do it. I prayed that her father who had long since passed away had greeted her at heaven's gate. Although her death was violent, I knew she had no more pain for an eternity. . . . I was grateful for this shared moment with her as I thanked the medical examiner personnel. I spent the remainder of the morning in the company of my family attempting to understand, almost demanding to know why? This question still haunts me and my family for what I believe to be the rest of our lives.

Bobby wrote that he believed his wife's death was an accident. She was not suicidal; she was happy and joyful in her life with her newborn son. She had no reason to take her own life. That knowledge would help him and the rest of Viki's devastated family though the coming hard times, he said. Did Viki ever suffer from depression? Yes, he wrote, after her father died several years earlier, she had been tormented by his death from cancer and often cried over how he never had the chance to experience the love of his grandson. Also, right after Monty was born, Bobby wrote that Viki was bedridden for two months, and he was the one who took time off from work and catered to the baby's every need. Even holding him in bed was extremely painful for Viki, and though she remained positive about the situation, it depressed her, Bobby said contradictorily.

Viki herself was ill for much of the last several years of our marriage. She suffered from a condition which involved long moments (days) of fatigue, listlessness and an arthritic condition. She was also medically deemed a free-bleeder. When she had her monthly menstruation cycle, she would bleed unlike any woman I've ever known. . . . This was our major concern after we decided to have our child. We knew that the possibility existed that she would not survive childbirth. Incredibly, Monty's birth went extremely well. However, the doctor discovered that she was torn from the inside as he passed through her vaginal canal. Her vaginal canal suffered a four to six inch tear which required stitching. The doctor had mentioned that in all of her years in practice she had not seen another likened condition. On the follow-up visit soon after Monty's birth the gynecologist discovered that the stitches had torn and were no longer holding the vaginal wall intact. She did not order a second surgery fearing that Viki was too weak to survive it.

Despite these apparent health issues, however, Bobby ended his statement reinforcing Viki's love for Monty, and how she'd hoped to be a stay-at-home mother to her son. "He was a priority to her and she always made it known that he was her pride and joy."

CHAPTER 9

REACTION TO THE STATEMENT

What in the hell was that?

The Rangers read and reread Bobby Lozano's statement. It was the most bizarre document they had ever seen, they agreed. Who began telling about his wife's death by describing the meal and the wine they had twenty-four hours earlier? Who typed four single-spaced pages on the computer about the baby being sick and about his musings as he watched his wife swinging the child at the park? Who wrote phrases like "he giggled ever so mischievously as if to make sure that we knew that he knew we had left the house after he went to sleep"? If Tracy Murphree and Tony Bennie had wondered whether Bobby was involved in his wife's death, they wondered no more. Too many of his statements clashed with the physical evidence they already had seen at the crime scene. Too much of his story seemed odd, if not downright ludicrous. And this was coming from a police officer who knew what was needed in a statement, who had taken many statements himself. The police needed facts. Bobby had given them a complete load of bullshit.

For one thing, earlier he'd told them that Viki had been half sitting on the bed, leaning over her left knee. Now, his statement had her lying on her stomach. He'd supposedly pulled her up, and then she fell back. How come there was no blood on him when the paramedics arrived?

Bobby waited in another room. When they were finished going over his statement, they asked him if they could take the computer from his bedroom office. He agreed. They followed his car from Murphree's office to the house on La Mancha. At one point, both cars came to a stop sign on a street near Bobby's house. As they sat there, a woman passed by on her evening run.

"This little blonde came jogging by," the Ranger remembers. Bobby's car was in front, and Murphree and Bennie's car was behind it. "We watched him. His head turned as she went by, and he followed her out of sight with his eyes, just sitting there at that stop sign. His wife had been dead a couple of days, and he was checking out some other woman."

The Rangers met with Lieutenant Lee Howell the next morning and gave him a copy of Bobby's statement. They agreed that they now had enough discrepancies to consider the case a murder investigation. They made a list of potential witnesses and decided that no one but the detectives actively working the case—Sergeant Steve Macsas, Detective Jeff Wawro and themselves—would know what was happening.

Howell was floored. He had begun Saturday night thinking he had an accidental shooting or perhaps a suicide on his hands. A few things at the scene had bothered him, including Bobby's standoffish attitude, but he had not been willing to consider him a murderer. But now, this statement—he read and reread it. What was he to make of such a document? The way Bobby said he found his wife simply did not make sense given the way she was lying when paramedics arrived. He said he'd performed CPR on her, yet he could hardly have touched her—and a cop is trained to continue CPR once it is started until paramedics arrive and take over. And anyone who knew what they were doing, like a cop, would have pulled her off the bed to perform the procedure on a hard surface. And while Bobby claimed to have pulled Viki up and massaged her chest, there was no blood on him anywhere.

And then there was the mess with Cindy Waters. Howell knew this case was going to put a real blot on the reputation of the police department and his detective department in particular. He hated that.

Howell's telephone had begun to ring that Monday morning. Friends of Viki's, mothers of her piano students and her fellow schoolteachers all wanted him to know some things about Bobby that made them suspicious.

Bobby was really controlling of Viki, they said. Bobby had affairs. Viki had been happier since she had the baby than they had ever seen her, and there was no way she would have committed suicide and left her little boy motherless.

———————

Viki's funeral was on Wednesday at St. Andrew Presbyterian Church, the same church she had been married in sixteen years earlier. It was packed with family, friends, teachers and police officers. Detective Benny Parkey was among the mourners. He and Bobby had been partners for two years, and he'd actually come to the house on La Mancha the night of Viki's death when he heard what was happening, to offer his support as a friend. But when he'd tried to talk to Bobby, he'd gotten little response. Bobby had avoided him, Parkey thought. He'd seen him avoiding other officers as well. Even so, Parkey intended to seek him out after the funeral and offer to help any way he could. Parkey stood outside the door as the family filed out. He saw Bobby walking his way and prepared himself to greet him. But Bobby turned away, failing to meet Parkey's eyes, and walked in another direction. Parkey thought it was deliberate.

———————

Chris Kerner sat with some of Viki's other teacher friends at the funeral. She watched Bobby. She watched Viki's mother, Anna Farish. Anna shed tears. Bobby did not. Viki's brother, David Farish, rose to speak about his sister.

He recounted a Christmas when his sister told her husband she either wanted a baby or a puppy. Bobby ran right out and bought her a puppy, David said in an apparent attempt at humor.

That's not funny, Kerner thought. *That's so out of place.* It just reiterated that Bobby hadn't wanted children and she had. Viki must have gotten pregnant without his permission, Kerner assumed.

Chris Kerner had worked with Viki for fourteen years at Hodge Elementary School until Viki changed schools a year before she died. Kerner didn't like Bobby. She didn't like the way he'd brought Viki's tiny lunches to school and weighed her at the gym. She didn't like the way Viki became quiet when Bobby was around. She didn't like the way he smeared on the charm to the other women around the lunch table. He might be a ladykiller, Kerner thought, but he did nothing for her.

Chris Kerner worked out at the same gym as the Lozanos, and she noticed how Bobby strutted around the gym, looking at himself in the mirror, while Viki spent her time trying to please him with perfection in her form with the weights.

Kerner had learned of Viki's death while she was attending a baseball game. Her sister-in-law called with the terrible news. She walked out to her car and sat staring at her telephone.

Oh my God. This has really happened. He's done it.

Years later, she realized that Viki fit the profile of an abused woman, though Kerner didn't know the signs at the time. "I feel so guilty," she lamented. "Maybe there was something I could have said or done that would have changed things."

———————

Denton lawyer Rick Hagen showed up in Lieutenant Howell's office the day after the funeral. Hagen was a bit of a superstar in Denton County law enforcement circles. He was known for getting cases dismissed before they ever came to the courtroom or pulling miraculous plea bargains out of a hat if they did.

Bobby had retained him the day before, Hagen said. Howell wondered if that had been before or after he attended his wife's funeral service. Hagen brought a half-page supplement to Bobby's original statement, which included the information about Cindy Waters. He'd met with Tony Bennie and Tracy Murphree on July 8, Bobby wrote in the supplement, in order to answer questions about the death of his wife: He changed his story about the night before Viki's death.

I stated that after my wife and I had returned home from dinner, she and I played with our son for a while. After we had returned him to bed, I advised that my wife and I retired to our bedroom and soon fell asleep. This was incorrect.

Bobby wrote that he had failed to mention he'd actually left the house after midnight. He'd told Viki that he needed to go to the office to catch up on paperwork, he said. She wasn't happy but asked that he not work too late, since they had plans to take Monty to the park early the next morning.

After I left, I drove to Cindy Waters' home. I stayed there approximately two hours. Afterward, I returned directly home. I remained there until the following morning when Monty awoke. I did not include this detail in the original written statement unwilling to involve details of an affair which I had been having with her.

"When can he come back to work?" Hagen asked.

"There's no hurry. Tell him to take as much time as he needs. Tell him to call when he feels ready, because if the investigation has been concluded by then we may want him to attend a counseling session before he returns to duty."

A week later, the supervisor over the police records department visited Howell in his office. There had been an open records request from a man named Kenny Johnson for the 911 tape. Howell told the supervisor, as per policy, to refer the request to the city attorney's office. Johnson turned out to be an investigator for Hagen. The city attorney notified Johnson that the tape was part of an ongoing investigation and would not be released.

Rick Hagen was a hometown guy, but when he'd graduated from high school, his aim hadn't been to become a lawyer. He loved the rodeo and was a bareback rider on the circuit. By 1985 he had attained full membership in the prestigious Professional Rodeo Cowboys Association. But in 1986, an injury ended that career and he looked around for something just as challenging. He settled on the law.

He earned an undergraduate degree from Austin College and worked as a legislative assistant for State Representative Jim Horn. He obtained a law degree from the University of Oklahoma and went to work as a briefing attorney for the Texas Court of Appeals, the highest criminal court in Texas. He worked as a prosecutor for a couple of years, but in 1993 he returned to his hometown and joined the law practice of Hal Jackson, one of the most respected and successful defense lawyers in the county. He married and had two children. He lived on a ranch inside Denton city limits, and his young daughter was proving her prowess as a horsewoman.

Jackson, who had hired Hagen at the beginning of Hagen's law career, had a photographic memory. He had loved to glance at the jury panel list, look at the jurors and then begin calling them by their names without referring to the list as he questioned them in voir dire. Jackson had a reputation for finding a way to stay out of the courthouse, for getting his defendants off without having to face a jury. And failing that, for dazzling jurors with his courtroom skills. Soon, that reputation rubbed off on Hagen too.

Known as a good lawyer to retain when a law enforcement officer got into trouble, Hagen had worked a plea bargain for another Denton officer who had swindled an elderly woman out of thousands of dollars. The officer resigned when he was indicted. The plea involved him giving up his law enforcement license and paying back the money. People wondered whether Hagen would be able to keep Bobby out of trouble. At first, it looked as though the Lozano case was going to be a star in Hagen's crown, but it didn't turn out that way.

Cindy Waters called Lieutenant Howell on Friday. She had remembered some things that were bothering her, she said. A week before Viki's death she and Bobby had gone shooting at the range. He had handed her his pistol and told her to try it out. Her fingerprints might be on the gun! She also said that during that late night or early morning visit Friday into Saturday, Bobby had asked her to again visit the range with him. She'd said no.

She wondered if he'd been trying to set her up.

Howell remembered that Bobby had also claimed that he and his wife had plans to go to the range that day.

Three days later, Cindy Waters brought in a twenty-nine page handwritten statement to Howell. It was much like her earlier two written statements except it had more detail and contained many of her fears and concerns about her affair with Bobby and what that might've meant in the death of his wife.

In the days after the shooting, Cindy Waters waffled back and forth about whether she was really afraid of Bobby and afraid for Viki after Bobby told her about the substance in the white bottle he said was some sort of poison. She wrote in her statements that the things he said earlier about "accidents do happen" were said in jest. But her friend Jackie, who had listened to hours of Cindy's talk about Bobby, told police that Cindy was really afraid. On July 16, 2002, Cindy called to admit she really had been afraid for Viki and now she was afraid for herself and her children. *Are we in danger?* she asked Howell. He told her he didn't think so, but that she should consider having the locks changed on her doors.

———————

Lieutenant Howell, Detective Wawro and the Rangers met with members of the Tarrant County Medical Examiner's Office on July 24, 2002, in Fort Worth. They learned the gun had been fired from three to six inches away from the victim's chest. Tests for gunshot residue were positive along Viki's sleeves. The exit wound was "shored," the pathologist said, meaning she had been lying on her left side against a firm surface when shot, causing a sort of lip around the wound and allowing the bullet to come to rest inside her pajama top. The angle of the bullet was about forty-five degrees downward. Transfer blood had been found on the bottom of the oilcan, meaning that it had been touched by a bloody hand.

There was no gun oil found on Viki's hands or clothing. Given the oily surface of the gun from one end to the other, it was clear that she hadn't touched the gun that killed her.

"There is nothing to rule out homicide," Dr. Gary Sisler, the pathologist who performed the autopsy, told them.

But the pathologist wasn't ready to release his findings yet. The group agreed to meet again on August 14.

The Rangers began searching for other girlfriends. They confirmed four others and talked to several women rumored to have had affairs with Bobby who stoutly denied it. They took statements from Cindy and the other four women. Some of the things they learned simply amazed them. For example, Bobby claimed to have poisoned two dogs to test that method of putting Viki out of her supposed misery while suffering from the supposed leukemia. Did he really do that? Could he have been that cold? Viki did not have blood cancer, but her death was obviously on her husband's mind.

Another thing the Rangers noticed—all the women looked something alike, and they all resembled Viki. Bobby obviously had an affinity for slim, fit blondes. The more the Rangers talked to Bobby's women, the more they thought of him as a likely killer. The man had no compunction about killing dogs, according to his own stories, or unborn babies, given his preference for abortions when his girlfriends got pregnant. He seemed to enjoy making women cry. He was totally involved in what was best for Bobby, and he had no problem telling outrageous lies to get the tiniest thing he wanted. Bobby Lozano, they decided, was a psychopath.

Three weeks after Viki's death, Bobby resigned from the police department.

Lee Howell still hadn't heard anything from Viki's mother, Anna Farish. He thought it was time to tell her where the investigation was heading. He first called her son, David Farish, and asked him to come to the police department. Farish and his wife came by on July 27, 2002. Farish began by saying he knew that Bobby had resigned.

"Bobby told me the environment has become uncomfortable," Viki's brother said. *Uncomfortable?* Howell thought. Bobby would have faced an internal affairs investigation had he not resigned. Anything he said there would be used in court, and he would've been fired if they found that he lied. Yes, that would be uncomfortable if a man had killed his wife.

"Bobby prides himself on being the best, and he thinks he'd have trouble being accepted now," David Farish said. He added that he knew about the affair, and that Bobby had spoken to Anna about it as well.

"I don't know if Viki knew about it or not," her brother said. "But if she did, she would have tried to problem-solve it and work it out." Viki had been very happy almost since the day she became pregnant with Monty, he said. The couple's homelife had been very much improved since then.

He claimed that his sister had had a bedside gun of her own and was comfortable cleaning guns. "Viki could break down a gun and put it back together, probably better than Bobby could," David claimed.

However, officers never found another gun in the bedroom save Bobby's service pistol. And they never found any disinterested party who could corroborate whether Viki had any idea at all of how to clean a gun.

David also related a time when Viki, as a joke, had disassembled Bobby's gun and hidden a piece of it. For a police officer, a disabled gun is not a joke, Howell thought.

Bobby was often away from home because of his work with the FBI, David Farish told Howell. He said he knew "for a fact" that his brother-in-law worked often late into the night on an undercover job "busting high-volume criminals," and he was often called out on holidays. It was news to Bobby's supervisor.

Howell asked David to set up a second meeting, which would include his mother, Anna, and the two of them came to the police department on August 1, 2002. Howell asked Sergeant Steve Macsas to sit in on the meeting. Macsas had a soft touch and a way with women, and Howell thought he would be able to help keep the meeting on a level basis.

But Anna Farish came loaded for bear. She had no questions. She had only complaints and orders. She'd heard "horrible rumors" that Bobby was involved in her daughter's death, she said. The rumors had to be the fault of the police, and she wanted them stopped immediately. They were tearing her apart and were not fair to Viki or Monty. Bobby had received a text message that said, "They're calling Frank to the PD, and you're about to be arrested. Get your family prepared."

No, she didn't actually see the text, Anna said in answer to Howell's questions. Bobby had erased the text before he told her about it.

Bobby had told her about the affair but said he went to Cindy's house the night of his anniversary to put an end to it, Anna claimed. Early in the spring she had heard a message left on the house answering machine from Bobby. Apparently he had called home by mistake, she said. She thought he meant the message for another woman. After that she had watched him closely. There was no indication of any affair after that, she said.

"There is still much to do in this investigation," Howell said. "We're waiting on the medical examiner's report, but the possible outcomes would be either homicide, suicide or accidental death."

"The first two are unacceptable," Anna Farish said. In response to Howell's question about what she thought happened that night, Anna laid the blame on the family pets. "I think the dogs caused the gun to go off," she said. "One of them is old and not in good shape, and he might have gotten into a bind and Viki reached to help him and it went off."

Howell called Anna Farish a month and a half later, on September 16, 2002, to inform her they were close to getting a full medical examiner's report.

She was still hearing "ugly rumors" about Bobby, Anna said. She wanted Howell to declare her daughter's death an accident.

"I can't face bringing Monty up with that stigma or without either of his parents," she said.

A month later, Anna Farish called Howell, who had recently been promoted to captain. He still kept the case close despite his different and more elevated status. Howell remembers that Anna said she had heard a rumor that Bobby was going to be indicted soon. She said she didn't care about Bobby's affair; he and Viki had had a good marriage, she insisted. The case wasn't really being investigated by the Rangers as the police were telling everyone, she said, accusing the police department of conducting the investigation themselves because they were out to get Bobby.

As Howell later testified to the conversation, he was flabbergasted when she said, "When you came out to the car that night to get me I saw hate in your eyes. I'm not a well woman, and I don't know if I can take this."

He called Anna Farish on Monday, December 9. The case would be presented to a grand jury on Thursday, he told her.

"I know about grand juries," Howell testified that she told him. "My husband served on a grand jury. The district attorney can get them to do anything he wants them to do." Again, he said, she went on the attack, accusing, "You have not investigated this case properly. You have not talked to the right people."

Despite her earlier insistence that suicide was one of the "unacceptable" outcomes of the medical examiner's report, Anna now said that Viki had attempted suicide in the past. Bobby had told her about a couple of times when her daughter had tried to harm herself. She gave details of what Bobby had told her of finding Viki in the bathtub passed out, and of finding her in the garage with a gun barrel stuck in her mouth.

"If you knew about these things, why haven't you told us before now?" Howell asked Anna. "I asked you months ago what you really thought, and you said you thought the dogs jumped on the bed."

"I didn't want it to come out that Viki killed herself," she said. "It isn't fair for Monty to have to live with the idea that his mother killed herself. I wanted this to be an accident so no one would have to know the truth. I don't want anyone to know now who doesn't have to know."

She had no medical records to back up the suicide stories, she admitted.

Anna specifically asked that Detective Jeff Wawro, the lead investigator on the case for the police, not be told about her new suicide theory. She believed that Wawro, who was a building contractor on the side and had designed their house but not built it, was getting even with Bobby by accusing him of murder. Besides, Anna said, Wawro hated Bobby because of Wawro's strict religious beliefs. Howell wondered what religion Wawro might have embraced that *would* have encouraged adultery.

———

Finally, the autopsy report was ready. It contained the findings about the oil, the gunshot residue and the shored exit wound, among other things. But Dr. Gary Sisler told the officers that he felt that the forensic report alone would not prove the case a homicide. He really couldn't tell just by his own findings whether the case was homicide, suicide or accidental. He proposed ruling the manner of death "undetermined," and the officers were fine with that. It was a common determination unless there was a slam-dunk forensic case. It didn't mean that Sisler didn't think that Bobby killed his wife. In fact, he told them that the rest of the evidence made him certain they had a homicide on their hands.

"If Bobby Lozano didn't kill his wife, I'll grow hair on my head and marry a fifteen-year-old girl," the bald octogenarian said.

On December 12, 2002, Robert Cruz Lozano was indicted for the murder of his wife, Virginia Kaye "Viki" Lozano. He surrendered two days later at the county jail with his lawyer, Rick Hagen, at his side. Bail had been arranged ahead of time, though, so Bobby never had to approach a jail cell. He simply posted $125,000 bail and walked back out and home to his mother-in-law.

Four days later, Howell called David Farish. He wanted to meet with him and Anna to discuss elements of the case, he said. David said the family had expected Bobby to be indicted, but right now, they just wanted to get through the holidays. He would call after that, he said. David Farish did call on January 3, 2003. He said they were still thinking about whether to meet with the police. Howell didn't hear from him again.

Prosecutor Debra Bender was named "first chair" on the Lozano case by the district attorney. Prosecutor Tony Paul would assist her. Bender had been a felony prosecutor only a short time and had never prosecuted a murder case. The investigating officers were stunned and angry that someone so junior had been assigned to the case. At first, District Attorney Bruce Isaacks had said he would try the case himself, Howell recalls. Then First Assistant District Attorney Lee Ann Breading said it was the strongest circumstantial case she had ever seen, and she'd like to try it. So why had those two handed over a high-profile, difficult case to a beginner?

Howell never found out.

Years later, Texas Ranger Tracy Murphree freely gave his opinion of the neophyte prosecutor, which wasn't high.

"You have good prosecutors," he said. "And then you have Debra Bender."

After she was assigned to the case, he met with Bender only once, the Ranger said. She asked him only two questions about the case, neither one seemingly pertinent.

"She asked had I been drinking that night before I went to the Lozano house and I said no. And then she asked if I knew about any other affairs that were going on then with anyone else at the police department. What that had to do with the case, I don't know."

CHAPTER 10

THE INDICTMENT

After five months of waiting, I finally had my story. Sergeant Steve Macsas tipped me off that the grand jury would be considering the Lozano case that Thursday, December 12, 2002. I went up to the second floor of the courthouse around midmorning to lurk in the hallway and wait for the grand jury to file out and into the courtroom where the judge would read the indictments aloud. Grand jury proceedings are top secret. Witnesses may not divulge what goes on in there. Chief Bailiff Jim Bob Kline, the guardian of the grand jury room door, always got nervous when I hung around, but it was the only way to know when the indictments were about to be read in open court. Sometimes the officers waiting their turn to testify would talk to me about other cases, or about their wives or their dogs or the weather. But never about their testimony. Jim Bob watched us carefully.

Lieutenant Lee Howell and the two Texas Rangers were testifying before the grand jury. It had been scheduled as the last item on the agenda that day because it was likely to take a long time. I stood in the marble hallway in my high-heeled shoes until my feet complained. Then I sat on a chair around the corner in the jury selection area. But that meant I couldn't see the hallway in front of the grand jury room or the door to the staircase from there, and it made me nervous. Grand jurors often took the stairs to the floor where the judge overseeing the grand jury that term held court. So I walked back around the corner and leaned against the wall. Jim Bob frowned at me. I held my ground.

Finally, the jury filed out, all sixteen of them. As I'd suspected, they took the stairs to the third floor and Judge Jake Collier's 158th District Court. I jumped on the elevator and rode up, arriving just as the grand jurors were filing into the jury box. I couldn't read the looks on their faces. Rick Hagen, Bobby's lawyer, was already sitting in the courtroom. He acknowledged me with a nod. We waited. The judge finished his business and turned to Jim Bob, who handed him the pages of names and indictments representing that morning's work by the grand jury. He read through them quickly, and I had to strain to hear. The last name he read was Robert Lozano, indictment for murder. I took a hurried quote from Hagen and found the Rangers, who also gave me quotes. But as for real information, I had very little more than I did at the beginning.

I wrote a story leading with the indictment of Bobby Lozano for murder and filled it in with what little details I could find. Bobby appeared at the jail, bringing his lawyer and $125,000 surety from a bail bondsman that he would appear for trial, which probably cost his mother-in-law about $20,000. His mug shot appeared on the judicial system website. In the photo, he wore a yellow pullover shirt and looked relaxed.

He went back to whatever he was doing. I didn't know what that was. I went back to writing my daily stories, waiting for a trial date to be announced.

And then—nothing happened.

Some reporters got into the news business because they thought the work was glamorous. Wrong. Some became reporters because they thought they could save the world. This was also wrong, though occasionally journalists could make a small difference, and that's what they lived for. Some did it because they were nosy and had a bent for writing. That was me.

This case was driving me crazy. I had thought that once the indictment came down, things would loosen up and I would finally learn what the case was really all about. But it didn't happen.

Months went by, and no trial date was set. An entire year went by, and still no trial date. Whenever I saw Bruce Isaacks, the district attorney, I would ask him what was happening, but the answer was always the same: They were not ready to take the case to trial.

Bruce Isaacks had been district attorney of Denton County for a dozen years when he obtained the indictment against Bobby Lozano. He had a lot of clout in state government for a boy from Joshua, Texas. During his term that clout may have come into play when his boyhood friend and neighbor L. Dee Shipman snared the bench of a court newly created by the Texas Legislature. Isaacks's wife, Vicki, also was appointed to a judgeship in 1999. Vicki had been acting as counsel to a police department when the legislature picked her for Denton County's new 293rd District Court. But ultimately, her contentious administrative decisions on that bench, documented by investigative reports in the *Dallas Morning News* and complained about loudly by county commissioners, and the Isaackses' oldest son's criminal arrests likely later contributed to Bruce Isaacks's downfall.

I was frustrated about the time it was taking to get Bobby to a courtroom. My curiosity still had not been assuaged, and I knew the public's curiosity was still high as well. What could be taking so long? It was going on two years since Viki's death with no court date set. No one seemed to know except Isaacks, and he wasn't talking.

Denton police chief Charles Wiley also was frustrated. He met with Isaacks several times and was told there was more work to be done. Isaacks's investigators didn't seem to be finding any more evidence, so Wiley didn't know what the holdup could be.

Meanwhile, Bobby Lozano was seen around town with Cindy Waters. They were still dating, rumor had it, and people who claimed to know said that Cindy had become a surrogate mother to Monty, Bobby's baby boy. But Bobby dutifully went home to Anna, his mother-in-law, every night. He and Cindy were working as mortgage brokers, but Bobby was technically under indictment for Viki's murder, and he couldn't afford to offend the goose that laid the golden eggs. He wanted to live in the house he had designed totally to his own taste. He wanted to inherit it. And he needed the money to pay one of the most expensive lawyers in Denton—Rick Hagen.

Rick Hagen filed two motions in the spring of 2004. One was a motion to set a deadline of June 1 for the state to produce results of tests the state had supposedly asked for after a joint interview with the medical examiner who performed the autopsy. The judge granted that motion, stating that the tests had been completed and the results should be turned over to the defense.

The deadline passed. Then Hagen filed another motion. This was a motion to compel the state to turn over the test results, alleging that state lawyers claimed the medical examiner had not sent any results to them.

Dr. Gary Sisler would later testify that no further tests had ever been requested or performed. And evidence in that trial would show that no further tests existed in anyone's files. No one was ever able to explain where the idea of these supposed tests had come from.

I worked for a daily newspaper, and editors' attitudes were "What have you done for me today?" So, given the total lack of progress on the case, Bobby Lozano had moved to a back burner while other criminals committed their felonies and misdemeanors, trudging through the court system and out of the limelight.

Then, on July 24, 2004, a fax arrived at the newspaper,

addressed to me from the office of the district attorney, signed by first assistant Lee Ann Breading. It had been eighteen months since the indictment, and more than two years since Viki's death.

They were dropping the charges against Lozano.

Numbly, I read and reread the press release. It didn't make sense to me. Then I went to the courthouse and obtained a copy of the affidavit for the motion to dismiss.

Motion to dismiss

To the honorable judge of said court:

Now comes the State of Texas, by and through her Attorney, and respectfully requests the Court to dismiss the above entitled and numbered criminal action in which the defendant is charged with the offense of murder, for the following reasons:

In preparation for trial an attorney for the State of Texas was present during an interview of the individual from the Tarrant County Medical Examiner's Office who performed the autopsy on Virginia Lozano. Additionally, attorneys for the State of Texas have interviewed other members of the Tarrant County Medical Examiner's Office on multiple occasions since the Medical Examiner who performed the autopsy, Gary L. Sisler, D.O., now favors suicide as the manner of death as opposed to undetermined as initially stated in the autopsy report. Other members of the Tarrant

County Medical Examiner's Office now believe there is no credible evidence of homicide as a manner of death.

The State has consulted with the Chief Medical Examiner for Cook County, Illinois, who was hired to review the evidence in this case. In reviewing the evidence he found evidence that had been overlooked by the Tarrant County Medical Examiner's Office that supports a conclusion that the death was a result of suicide as opposed to homicide. Following the Cook County Medical Examiner's review of the evidence the State requested the Tarrant County Medical Examiner's Office to re-examine this evidence and conduct additional tests. The results of these tests were communicated to the Chief Medical Examiner for Cook County.

I paused right there to think. What medical examiner? No name was mentioned in the document. And why was he consulted? I was shocked, but I read on.

That Medical Examiner has informed the State that it is his conclusion by a preponderance of the evidence that the manner of death of Virginia Lozano was more likely suicide than homicide.

The State of Texas is unable to proceed given the current opinion of these witnesses. The State of Texas has insufficient evidence to present a prima facie case against Robert Lozano at this time and requests that this case be dismissed.

It was signed by Bruce Isaacks, criminal district attorney.

Why another medical examiner? I asked Breading. And why one from Chicago? She would not tell me. I sent a written request to the Tarrant County medical examiner, Dr. Gary Sisler, for a statement on the dismissal. His written answers indicated that not only had he not changed his mind about Viki's manner of death, but that he had *not* changed the official manner of death result. I didn't know what to make of that. I called Dr. Edmund Donaghue in Chicago and questioned him about his finding that Viki's death was suicide. He was vague on the phone and would not tell me what the overlooked evidence had been. He had very little at all to say about the statement he supposedly made that caused a murder indictment to be dropped. I was puzzled. And when I called Lieutenant Lee Howell for a quote about the dismissal, he was taken by surprise. There had been talk earlier of dropping the indictment, but no one at the district attorney's office had notified Denton police before they sent out the press release that their murder case was being dismissed.

I called Dr. Nisam Pierwani, the medical examiner in charge of the Denton County office. He was out of the country and could not be reached. I had to write what I could confirm that night, but I wasn't happy. Something felt wrong. Why had the district attorney contacted a seemingly random medical examiner in another part of the United States? Why then? Why him? How could he make a judgment different from the original pathologist when the only thing he had to go by was that pathologist's report? I wasn't getting answers.

I got generic statements from Howell and from police chief Charles Wiley. They had presented their best case to the district attorney, they said. They were disappointed, but they had to abide by the decision of the DA. Despite their polite statements, however, I felt an undercurrent of outrage from them both and from the whole department, though no one would voice that outrage on the record. Police don't openly buck the district attorney.

Texas Ranger Tracy Murphree heard about the dismissal from Jeff Wawro, lead detective on the case. The DA was saying the case was not winable because the two medical examiners now believed it was suicide, Wawro told him. Murphree was strongly disappointed. But it did not occur to him to question the truth of that statement.

"I should have picked up the telephone and called Sisler," he said later. "But I tend to believe the DA when he makes a statement. I was good with dropping the case because we couldn't win it."

Sisler was furious. He told friends that he planned to file a grievance against Isaacks with state authorities. But politics may have intervened. According to Sisler, Dr. Nisam Pierwani didn't want to pursue trouble with Isaacks.

Pierwani worked in a complicated contract with Tarrant County. Instead of being hired as an employee of the county, he formed his own company, and that company worked under contract for the medical examiner services for Tarrant County. He paid his employees from company funds. In turn, Denton County contracted with Tarrant County for medical examiner services. Isaacks had already been making noise about Denton County's need for its own medical examiner and lab. Presumably, Pierwani didn't want to rock the boat. No formal objection ever came from his office. Sisler remained angry, but he kept quiet.

The case was officially dead. Bobby Lozano would not face trial for the death of his wife. He continued to live with Anna Farish—who, it soon became obvious, was not only his benefactor but his staunchest defender—and his small son in the house where Viki died.

Everyone said there was nothing to do about it. But I wondered. There were so many questions unanswered. So much strangeness from the beginning to the conflicting stories about the medical examiner's change of mind about the manner of death. Nothing changed on the public website. The cause of death remained "undetermined" on the list.

And I did not forget Viki, who didn't live to see the first birthday of the little boy she had waited so long for. Who didn't get to see him take his first steps. My curiosity was as strong as ever about what had really gone on in that room the night that a baby lost his mother; a woman lost her daughter and seemingly didn't care; and a lovely young woman lost her life. I would keep trying to find the truth, I silently vowed to the woman I had never known in life. I felt her close to me now. I felt her pain. I began to believe that I was the only one who cared about her.

It later turned out that I was wrong about being the only one who remembered her. Viki remained a sore spot in the hearts of many of her schoolteacher friends. She was a point of regret for the police officers who worked the crime scene that night. Could they have done something different? Better? Certainly, they made mistakes that night, they admitted among themselves. Should they have treated Bobby as a suspect instead of a coworker, a friend? Absolutely. But hindsight is perfect, and they didn't know when they were processing the scene some things they learned later. And it was too late by then to go back, they thought.

But maybe it wasn't.

CHAPTER 11

BOBBY AND CINDY

Cindy Waters had been put on paid administrative leave after she confessed to the affair with Bobby Lozano. She believed she could stay on the force when everything was straightened out. Then she received formal notice of an internal affairs investigation. If she were fired, she could never be a police officer anywhere else because her record would bear that firing. Her only alternative was to resign before the investigation. Regretfully, she submitted her resignation.

She had been a child abuse investigator, and a good one, her coworkers said. She'd not only worked her current cases, but she'd kept up with the children involved in previous cases. She gave them a code word. When she called to see how they were doing, they could use the code word to let her know they were being abused again. After leaving her job, Cindy worried about those kids. She felt like she had abandoned them. Who would protect them now? She'd loved her career, and not only was it gone, but it had crashed in disgrace. She felt shame and guilt to the point that she could barely function. And fear for what was going to happen. Her former fellow officers treated her like a suspect. No one would tell her anything about the crime itself, and initially, she stayed away from Bobby. She was confused. Had he killed Viki, as everybody was saying?

Texas Ranger Tony Bennie interviewed her in Lieutenant Lee Howell's office. He accused her of knowing more than she was admitting about the death of her lover's wife. He accused her of lying. Cindy stormed out of Howell's office in tears, but the lieutenant came after her and convinced her to return. Later, she brought a long handwritten statement to Howell containing her every thought and fear about Bobby and the case.

One late night someone knocked on her door. It was Bobby. She let him in. He was very convincing. He wanted to resume their relationship. He wanted to take her to his lawyer, Rick Hagen. Hagen would explain everything, Bobby said. All her questions would be answered, and she would realize that he had not killed his wife.

"You know you had nothing to do with Viki's death, yet they suspect you," he said. "That is the same thing that is happening to me."

It made sense. Cindy agreed to meet with Hagen. She sat down with the two of them, and they convinced her that Bobby was a victim of a vindictive plot to convict him of a crime he didn't commit. The two men were particularly concerned that she understand about an L-shaped bruise between Viki's eyes. Anna Farish, Bobby claimed, had gone to the police and signed an affidavit that explained how Viki had stumbled and hit her forehead on the corner of a coffee table.

It was only years later that Cindy learned that everything Bobby told her then was a lie. That the bruise they told her Anna had explained away had actually only showed up after Viki's body was taken to the coroner's office. It was that fresh. Years later she learned that Anna had never gone to the police or signed any kind of affidavit. But she didn't know it then, and Bobby and his lawyer had explained away all her fears.

So Cindy and Bobby began to see each other again. And once more her hopes rose for the fairy-tale ending she had dreamed about. Bobby often brought over his little boy, Monty. She was going to be his mother, he said, and he wanted them to bond.

Monty was happy to spend time with Cindy and her two boys. He loved to play with their trucks. He loved to dig worms in the yard with them. Cindy bought him cute T-shirts with Superman and SpongeBob SquarePants on the front when she bought them for her boys. Bobby didn't like the T-shirts—he dressed his son as he did himself, always in dress clothes, never blue jeans. Bobby never looked casual. He was always dressed to kill.

Viki's death never left Cindy's mind for long. But Bobby wouldn't talk about it. If she brought it up, he became upset. He cried.

"If it weren't for me and you, she would be alive today," he would tell her.

It was only later that Cindy realized that he was using her feelings of guilt to stop her questions.

Bobby had a lot of cash. He bought her presents. He bought things for her rented house outside of Denton. Bobby wanted only the best, she knew. And the things in her house were not good enough for him. He explained the cash by telling her that he had refinanced his house to help pay his attorney fees. Cindy never knew that he owned the house with Anna, his mother-in-law. She never knew that he actually sold Anna his half, and that was where the cash came from.

Cindy and Bobby started a mortgage broker business together, but Cindy did all the complicated paperwork for the mortgages because, in reality, Bobby didn't know how to fill out the forms and didn't want to learn. She was confused when he later asked her to handle another refinance for his house. The paperwork showed only Anna's name on the deed, and it didn't show a prior refinance. What was going on?

Despite a few red flags, though, when the indictment against Bobby was dropped, Cindy felt her faith in him had been justified. Bobby must be innocent, she thought, or else the district attorney would not have dropped the charges. They could begin to really live again. Bobby gave her an engagement ring, and they started building a new house together. His taste, from the beginning, exceeded their budget. He paid five thousand dollars for the front door. They argued over his spending on the house, but he continued his extravagant ways.

One day they were out at the building project. The rooms had been framed in. The three boys were skipping from room to room, picking out which would be their own.

"We'll have a playroom upstairs, and there will be no toys downstairs," Bobby told the boys.

No toys downstairs? Cindy thought. These were little boys. Did he not understand how children were? Monty never got to be a kid unless he was at her house, she realized. He was never allowed to get dirty. His father took his little outfits to the cleaners to be starched.

Almost from the day he gave her the engagement ring, Bobby changed. No more was he the romantic, over-the-top lover she'd known. He wasn't around much. He never spent the night at her house. Often now, he brought Monty for her to "bond" with and then left. Slowly, as the romance drained out of their relationship, it dawned on her.

I am the babysitter. I am Viki. He is romancing someone else, and I'm the one at home. He has to have a wife, and he has to have a girlfriend. Now, I'm the wife and he has another girlfriend.

He rarely was at the office they shared downtown in their mortgage broker business. He said he was working at home, but Cindy wondered where he really was. One evening they left the house building project together, and she had all three boys with her. She thought Bobby was following right behind. But he didn't arrive at her house. Monty was upset. He wanted his daddy. Where was his daddy?

Bobby wasn't answering his telephone. Cindy was upset too, but she tried not to show it to the boys.

Finally, late at night, Bobby returned her many messages.

"Where are you?" she asked.

"I'm at home."

"Monty is upset. He thought you were coming right along. I did too. I thought you were spending the night. He's crying."

Bobby drove to her house and picked up his son.

"Where were you? Why didn't you answer your phone? What is going on?" she asked.

Bobby looked at her. His eyes were hard. He was not the Bobby she had ever seen before.

"Don't you question me," he said. "You have no idea what I'm capable of." He left.

Chills rose all over her. For the first time, she was afraid of Bobby Lozano.

Cindy's world was spinning out of control. She begged him to come to couple's counseling with her. He refused. They yelled at each other on the phone, and he hung up. She didn't hear from him for several days. Then late one night, he called. He told her that he had a gun in his mouth, that he'd been victimized by the police, and now by her. Then he hung up and would not answer her frantic calls.

Finally, she left a message. "Call me back or I'm calling your family and the police."

He called. "I just need time," he said. "There are times when I just need to be alone."

That wasn't going to work for Cindy. She knew his times "alone" were with another woman. She gave him back the engagement ring.

But Cindy still loved him, though she no longer trusted him. She felt that she no longer knew who he really was. The more emotional distance she got from him, the more she realized what a little Stepford wife she had become under his thumb. Her nails always had to be perfect for him. Her makeup always had to be flawless.

One day, she arrived at work—they were still in business together—to find a package on her desk. Inside were copies of the district attorney's case file in the murder charge against Bobby. She had never seen any of the documents. There was no indication of who sent the files, and she never learned. She sat down and read them. Then she went into the bathroom and threw up.

Bobby had told her that he'd pulled Viki's body to the floor and tried to perform CPR. Now she learned that Viki's body had actually been left on the bed, and that no one believed Bobby had ever even tried the lifesaving measure. In the first place, only four minutes had elapsed between the time he told a dispatcher he was starting CPR to the time paramedics found him, spotless, standing in the front doorway holding Monty. There was nothing in the file about Anna cooperating with the police and signing an affidavit that Viki had hit her head, causing the L-shaped bruise. Instead, she learned that Anna had pretty much refused to cooperate at all. Anna believed that Bobby was innocent and she was not about to help the police with an investigation against him. Anna believed the police were trying to frame her beloved son-in-law. Cindy learned that almost everything Bobby told her had been a lie.

Cindy now believed without a doubt that Bobby Lozano had murdered his wife.

She was terrified. If he looked into her eyes again, he would know that she knew. Cindy was convinced of that. He had always been able to read her. He would do it this time—and then what would he do? All the lies that he had told her to keep her on his side had been revealed. He could no longer count on her to testify in his favor if the case ever came up again. If he found that out, what would happen?

Cindy's secretary could see the front door of the building from her office. Cindy told her to signal if she saw Bobby coming in the front door. When he arrived, Cindy scurried out the back door. She couldn't let him see her and realize that she knew.

One day she received a message from Bobby inquiring if she'd had fun in her camo outfit at a Halloween party. The only place she had talked about that costume was in the office. Was he bugging her phone? The entire office? Paranoia grew.

Then an e-mail came from him that sent her reeling. It was written as though it were her obituary. The strange message had the desired effect. She was terrified. When she drove up to her house that evening, she saw that the back door had been kicked in. Nothing was disturbed, but Bobby called her twenty minutes later. She should take care, he told her in a patronizing voice. This was a bad time for break-ins.

He wanted her to be afraid of him without actually threatening her.

Cindy did a lot of thinking about that last week before Viki's death. She remembered with alarm when Bobby had taken her to the shooting range. They had identical Glocks. But he had a new scope on his, he told her. He'd insisted that she try it out. Was he trying to get her fingerprints on the gun? She remembered that in the days before Viki's death, Bobby had carried a different gun in a shoulder holster to work. Had he been preserving her fingerprints on his weapon? Was she supposed to have been the one who had killed Viki? She was the girlfriend. She was sad at the time. She was emotional. Maybe Bobby had planned for Anna to find Viki that night. For police to find the Glock with Cindy's fingerprints on it. Maybe something went wrong at the last minute and that was the reason the staged crime scene was so sloppy. Bobby would have done it right. It would have been perfect, just like everything he did. But maybe, just maybe, something ruined his plan and he didn't have the proper time to fix it. He knew about lividity and that time was the key element. If Bobby's plan had worked, would Cindy be sitting in prison right now?

In a terrified rush to get away from him, Cindy packed up and moved to Tennessee.

CHAPTER 12

WAITING FOR THE MURDER BOOK

In the months that turned into years after the indictment, I only heard rumors about what Bobby Lozano was up to. A couple of years later, someone saw him at city league baseball games. He had a new girlfriend, not Cindy Waters, but she too looked a lot like Viki. No one seemed to know where he was living. County records showed he'd sold his part of the La Mancha house to Anna Farish. I searched his name regularly in the county records websites but did not find more property belonging to him. I did find a lawsuit. An insurance company sued him to avoid paying a $300,000 life insurance policy on Viki. If Viki committed suicide, the company's lawyer argued, the company did not have to pay because the policy had not been in effect long enough to supersede the policy against paying off on a suicide. If Bobby killed her, he should not benefit financially from that crime. The judge appointed a lawyer to represent Monty's interests. After mediation, Bobby's and Monty's lawyers received nearly $100,000. Monty received the rest, to be held in trust until his eighteenth birthday and overseen by his attorney. Bobby could not touch the money. He received nothing from the smaller policy. But the larger insurance policy for a million dollars paid off like a slot machine. Apparently, however, it didn't take Bobby long to go through a cool million.

Bruce Isaacks had been soundly defeated in the last election for district attorney. Part of Isaacks's unpopularity was of his own doing. Some in law enforcement had begun to perceive him as a district attorney who looked for reasons not to take cases. His handling of the Lozano case made political enemies among the police. His prosecutors were likewise occasionally perceived as lawyers who would rather just plead cases out and stay out of the courtroom. He was the subject of an investigative probe by reporters at the *Dallas Morning News* that showed a link between some high-profile cases he dropped and campaign contributions he received. But no actual wrongdoing was ever established.

Paul Johnson, a former prosecutor whom Isaacks had fired, was elected. He brought a big broom to the office and fired twenty-five lawyers. The landscape changed drastically in the office that took up half the third floor and half the fourth floor of the Denton County courthouse.

There was talk around the police department of reviving the Lozano murder case. There's no statute of limitations on murder. Lozano had not been tried, so double

Viki Lozano clowns at a school Christmas program for her fifth-grade students the year before her death. *Cristy Kerner*

Viki holds her infant son, Monty, a few months before her death. He was eleven months old when she was murdered in her bed as he slept in his crib across the house. *Cristy Kerner*

TOP RIGHT: Bobby served as best man at his friend and coworker Richard Godoy's wedding. Godoy testified during the trial that Bobby once asked permission to date his intern, to which Godoy said he replied, "Well you know, married men don't usually date." *Richard Godoy*

LEFT: Viki and Bobby, together on a couch at Godoy's wedding reception. Godoy testified that Bobby's distress seemed insincere when his wife's body was discovered, and that Bobby began asking about burial arrangements before Viki's body was even removed from the bedroom. *Richard Godoy*

Bobby poses with other members of the Denton police SWAT team. According to testimony he often used team callouts as an excuse to get out of the house to visit his girlfriends.
Denton Police Department

Cindy Waters—Bobby called her Sin—was one of Bobby's many girl-friends. She believed that he and Viki were getting an amicable divorce and that she and Bobby would then marry. *Richard Pruitt*/48 Hours

Karen Algrim, another girlfriend, testified against Bobby during the first day of his murder trial. She became pregnant during their affair, she said, and he talked to the embryo and called it "Monty." Then he paid for an abortion. *Richard Pruitt*/48 Hours

Viki's mother, Anna Farish, was a staunch supporter of Bobby's. She testified that he had saved her daughter's life by marrying her, and that he could never have killed her. She also testified that Viki often cleaned Bobby's Glock semiautomatic pistol while lying in bed. *Richard Pruitt/48 Hours*

Bobby designed this 5,000-square-foot house on La Mancha Street himself and continued to live there with his mother-in-law after Viki's death. Later he brought his girlfriend, Renee, to live there too, along with her three children. *Donna Fielder*

Bobby and Renee married shortly before Bobby's trial for the murder of his first wife began. The two brought a big Bible to court every day.
Al Key/Denton Record-Chronicle

LEFT: Renee sat in the front row behind Bobby every day, and learned the details of Viki's death. She had believed that Bobby already had been tried and found not guilty of Viki's death before she met him. *Richard Pruitt*/48 Hours

BELOW: Bobby's sister, Blanca, was several years older than Bobby and was always protective of her baby brother. She supported him during the trial and provided support for Renee as well. *Richard Pruitt*/48 Hours

Texas Ranger Tracy Murphree led the investigation, since Denton police did not want a possible conflict if they tried to investigate the case themselves. *Tracy Murphree*

Three hundred and sixty second district judge Bruce McFarling presides over the trial. *Richard Pruitt*/48 Hours

Husband-and-wife prosecutor team Cary and Susan Piel confer during a break in the trial. *Richard Pruitt*/48 Hours

Susan Piel examining a witness. Viki's brother, David Farish, watches from the front row behind her. *Richard Pruitt*/48 Hours

Cary Piel objects to a question asked by defense attorney Rick Hagen in cross examination. *Richard Pruitt*/48 Hours

Bobby and his lawyer, Rick Hagen, confer during the trial.
Richard Pruitt/48 Hours

ABOVE: Bobby sits with Hagen's assistant, Sarah Roland. *Richard Pruitt*/48 Hours

LEFT: Bobby's mug shot after his arrival at a unit of the Texas Department of Criminal Justice. His head was shaved and, deprived of the eyebrow waxing he favored earlier, his brows were growing back in when the mug shot was taken.
Texas Department of Criminal Justice

jeopardy did not apply. He could be indicted again, if the new district attorney could be talked into taking the case back to another grand jury. So Denton police lieutenant Roger White, who oversaw the criminal investigation division after the departure of Parkey, Howell and Macsas to the sheriff's office, talked to officials in the district attorney's office. He tried to convince them to at least look at the evidence. But he hit a wall. If there hadn't been enough evidence for Isaacks to try the case, there was no reason for them to try, they said. White firmly believed that Lozano had killed his wife. He didn't want him to get away with it. But like the others, he didn't know how to move the case back into the courthouse. It looked like the case was truly dead. White had known Bobby well. He had worked with him. He believed with all his heart and mind that Bobby murdered his wife. He hated to think of him getting away with it. But he didn't know of anything else to do to restart the case. It rested with the district attorney. And the district attorney wasn't interested.

I, however, couldn't let it go. No one could or would explain to me about the two medical examiners, and no one except me seemed to question it. I requested a copy of the autopsy report. It still came to the conclusion that the cause of Viki's death could not be determined by looking at the evidence from the body. But it pointed out some strong evidence that Viki did not kill herself. The gun was dripping in oil, it read, but Viki's hands were clean. There were unexplained bruises on her head and body. Sisler had not changed his mind about the cause of death. But he kept quiet. He would have told the law enforcement officers had they asked. But they didn't. They took the district attorney at his word.

I made another round of asking questions in the summer of 2008. If nothing was going to happen, why shouldn't I be allowed to see the files, I asked. But we might want to try again sometime, I was told. And we don't want all the evidence in the papers, they said.

"It's been four years since the indictment was dropped, and I've been patient and tried to work with you," I told Detective Sergeant Jim Brett. "I'm tired of waiting."

He nodded understandingly. He had not seen those files himself. No one had since Wawro sealed them and wrote that no one should touch them. The men in charge of the Lozano case had moved to the sheriff's office. The officers in charge now knew very little. Brett, for instance, had been a traffic sergeant. He knew what he believed, but he had not been privy to the case file. He would like to see Bobby have a day in court, Brett said. He would see what he could do. So he made some telephone calls, and a day or two later he told me to make an open records request. Johnson, the district attorney, when contacted by the police, had declared the case a dead issue.

I made the written request that day. I sent the message to the public information officer. He sent it to the correct officer to start the process. Apparently, there was a snag somewhere up the chain of command.

Almost two weeks later, Stephanie Berry, the lawyer for the police department, called me. "We're going to ask the attorney general if there's a reason to withhold the file," she told me.

"Well, you know, it's been twelve business days since I sent the open records request," I told her. "I was supposed to have an answer within ten days."

There was a long silence, then Berry finally said that the request had only landed on her desk a day earlier. She hadn't looked at the date and just assumed it was new. She said she'd call me back. A few minutes later, she did.

"OK," she said. "You're getting the files. It will take a few days to go through them. I'll get back to you."

City editor Matt Zabel looked around at me as I hung up and cheered. "I'm getting the files," I crowed.

He smiled. "All of them?"

"The whole box of them," I yelled.

No one else in the newsroom looked up from their computers. Newsrooms are quirky places. Reporters are a different breed. A cheer or a little yelling is not that unusual. It takes a barrage of cursing and screaming to attract much interest. And that happens about once a day.

Most of the lawyers involved in the original Lozano case were gone along with Isaacks and his first assistant, Lee Ann Breading. No one there apparently cared anymore whether the press looked at the evidence in the case or not. Ranger Tracy Murphree learned that I was getting the files from another officer who was not happy about the release of the evidence.

"I said, 'Good,'" Murphree remembered. "We're never gonna get him prosecuted, and at least he'll have people look him in the eye and know that he killed his wife."

It took a few days to get the file. Lieutenant Lee Howell and Jeff Wawro drove the few blocks from the sheriff's office to the police department and unsealed the box. Wawro, who now worked at the sheriff's office, had sealed it himself with orders written on the box to leave it sealed. They went through it, piece by piece, with Stephanie Berry. They marked items for redaction on copies. When they were done, every name in the file except for police officers was blacked out. But I was familiar with the case. I could fill in the blanks myself. And I didn't plan to use Bobby's mistresses' real names. They had been through enough. They were victims of a ladykiller.

Other media might want the files once they read my story, Howell told me. This way, if they had to give the files to anyone else, the witnesses would be protected. Just in case there ever was a trial. But no one believed there would be.

None of the precautions bothered me. The important thing was: I had the file!

I carried it to my house like the treasure it was and settled myself in to read it. That took preparation. I first wanted to read it all at once, like feasting on a whole pizza alone. Then I would read it again with a mind to what I would put in the newspaper story and what didn't need to be there. I would separate it into categories and lay it out on my dining table so my research could be handled economically. This research required concentration and room to work, neither of which I could have in the noisy newsroom. My editor understood that I would do this work at home.

That first night I had dinner, grabbed a cold drink and sat down in my favorite chair with the file in my lap. I remained there most of the night, mesmerized by the story that jumped off those pages.

It became clear very soon that Bobby considered himself a ladies' man. He considered women raw clay in his hands to shape into his preconceived image of the perfect female. He wanted a thin woman, blond, muscular in the way that women get when they work out fanatically. He wanted a certain style, a certain look of class. He wanted a pliable woman willing to be remade and willing to believe that he was a god among men and worth the wait for him to leave his wife, which never happened.

Five women gave written statements about their affairs with him. They were so similar, the same woman could have written all of them. Bobby wooed them. He wouldn't take no for an answer. He bought them jewelry and clothing to his taste. He bought them small appliances and decorative items for their homes. He put them on diets and worked out with them at the gym. He paid for haircuts and color—he liked honey blond. He sent flowers and cards. He sent long, romantic letters. He called and came by. He was good at giving sexual pleasure. He strung them along with promises until they either grew tired of waiting, figured out he was never going to leave his wife or gained weight, which heralded the end of his interest in them.

He told one of them that his wife was dying of blood cancer and that she had begged him to kill her. He told another that Viki was suicidal. The theme of those statements was clear: Viki Lozano's death was very much on Bobby's mind long before she actually died.

The full autopsy report, taken in the context of the whole case file, rocked me. Viki had bruises, some old, some so fresh they didn't show up until her body arrived at the coroner's office. There were old bruises on her legs and arms. No one knew what that meant. There were fresh bruises on her right hand and arm. There was an L-shaped bruise in the middle of her forehead. It could have been made by a blow from the butt of the Glock pistol. I began to picture a struggle. Could it have ended with a blow to the head and a shot while she lay unconscious on her side? How could Viki have fired the oily gun herself and avoided having oil on her hands and clothing? Where was the popcorn bowl she had obviously been eating from? And why would anyone, be it suicide or a gun-cleaning accident, shoot themselves while lying on their side?

And most of all—why did the district attorney drop this case?

I studied the documents for several days and then met with Lee Howell, who was now chief deputy at the sheriff's office. He brought his own files and some photographs from the death scene. If I were going to write a story, he said, he wanted me to have all the facts so the story would be correct and complete. He spent an afternoon filling in blank spots in my understanding and answering questions. And when we were done, I was ready to write the longest, most important newspaper story of my life.

Later I interviewed Dr. Gary Sisler, who was happy to

clear up his part in the dismissal of the case—which was none. He had had *no* part in the decision to drop the case, he said. He hadn't even known it was going to happen. He made his report in 2002. It was disputed in 2004. Now, in 2008, someone finally was going to lift the blame that Isaacks had laid at his feet. Sisler was grateful.

———————

One day I sat quietly at my desk and gathered my courage. I was going to call Anna Farish, and it was not going to be pleasant. I had learned by then that Bobby and Monty were living with her again, along with Bobby's latest girlfriend and her three children. Even for a house as large as that one, it had to have been crowded. It contained only three bedrooms, since Bobby had never intended for children in the house. I dialed the number, and Anna answered. I identified myself. I told her what I planned to do.

"You are not going to write a story about this. You are not going to bring it up again after all this time," she said.

"Yes, ma'am, I am. I wanted you to know ahead of time so you wouldn't be blindsided. I don't like to sneak up on people," I said.

"You must not have heard me," came the imperious voice. "I said you are not going to write that story."

This was the mother of a victim. This was an older woman. I did not want to be rude. But I needed her to understand.

"I'm sorry you are upset. But I am going to write the

story. I want to give you an opportunity for a comment," I said.

"I think you are way out of line doing this," she said and refused further comment.

Less than half an hour later my desk phone rang. The woman on the other end of the line identified herself as Renee Lozano. Renee said that she was Monty's stepmother. On the basis of the harm it would do for a six-year-old boy to have the scandal revived, she begged me not to write the story. There was nothing imperious about her; Renee seemed sincere, and she was unfailingly polite and nice. She told me that Bobby had been tried and found not guilty for the murder of his wife. Why would I want to bring that up?

No, I said. The case never went to trial. He was not found not guilty. I could tell she didn't believe me. I began to feel sorry for her. Here was another woman whom Bobby had lied to, and she was sleeping with him in the same room where Viki had died.

My investigative story ran Sunday, September 7, 2008. It began at the top of page one and jumped to fill page eleven. It took up all of page twelve and half of page thirteen. It was accompanied by head shots of Viki and Bobby Lozano, a computer rendition of the bedroom suite with the body's position on the bed, a timeline of events since their marriage and one of Bobby's smarmy love letters to Cindy Waters.

My telephone at home began ringing before 9 A.M. that day. The calls continued for days—weeks, really. Callers were congratulatory. They were outraged that Bobby was free. They were angry with Isaacks. They wanted to know what they could do to help bring a killer to justice.

Denton police officers were happy to see the truth published but were not hopeful that anything more would happen. Police see the rough side of life up close. It doesn't make for many optimists in the profession of law enforcement.

Ranger Murphree said he was upset when he read the quotes from the medical examiner. Dr. Sisler had never believed it was suicide, he was quoted as saying. He had never heard from the Chicago medical examiner, and he had never been asked to perform more tests. There *were* no more tests. The sworn affidavit signed by the district attorney was filled with lies.

"I felt deceived. I felt like I'd been lied to," the Ranger said. "Knowing that he did it and got away with it and I couldn't do anything about it—that hurt."

The long piece ran as the top story on the *Denton Record-Chronicle* website for days. The *Dallas Morning News* website linked to it so those readers had access as well. Comments under the story were harsh. Readers wanted Bobby to hang. They wouldn't mind if Isaacks swung alongside him. And the current district attorney, Paul Johnson?

"I told him, 'Paul, they say you have no balls,'" First Assistant District Attorney Jamie Beck told me. They were taking the case back to the grand jury, she said in an off-the-record conversation. They would do it before the month was out.

Tracy Murphree received a telephone call from prosecutor Cary Piel, who was considering taking on the case.

"Did Bobby kill her?" Piel asked.

"Absolutely," Murphree replied.

"Are you willing to go the distance with me?"

"Yes."

"Then we're going to do it."

That September 25 was my birthday. I spent most of it lingering in the uncomfortable halls of the Denton County Courthouse waiting for another grand jury to return with a verdict. I wasn't alone. Anna Farish sat at one end of the only bench in that end of the hallway. Bobby's attorney, Rick Hagen, sat at the other end. Neither spoke to me. I did not have the nerve to plop down between them, and Jim Bob Kline, the bailiff who watched over the grand jury, was wary of the situation. I paced the hallway, never getting out of sight of the people there, as Anna read something she had brought with her and Hagen thumbed through legal documents, both studiously ignoring me. Anna had come to talk to the jurors. She wanted to tell them that her son-in-law did not kill her daughter. The grand jury declined to listen to her. In Denton County, prosecutors presenting cases to the grand jury rarely call any witness other than the investigating officer.

The grand jurors had many questions for the three law enforcement officers. Howell, Bennie and Murphree were glad to answer every question.

"I answered them bluntly," Murphree said.

Finally, grand jurors left the jury room and filed into the courtroom on the floor above. Hagen was there, but Anna was not. Lee Ann Breading, Isaacks's assistant who had issued the initial press release about dropping the first indictment, was there. She was a defense lawyer now. Again, Bobby Lozano's name was last to be read. Again, he had been indicted for murder.

I buttoned my face tight. No one should see what I felt just then. It was pride. My story had rekindled something that everyone thought was dead. My determination had brought about nothing short of a miracle. But my parents had taught me that it was not nice to gloat. It was bad to brag about something you did. I kept my face expressionless.

I could see that Hagen was upset. The look he gave me was not pleasant. Breading walked up to him and gave him a hug. Given her role in the first case, it was shocking to see her tell him she was sorry. As a prosecutor, she had been a professional archenemy to defense lawyers. Now she worked on the other side. Even though Hagen would be paid handsomely for defending Bobby, Hagen's reputation lay in stopping the process before it reached the courtroom. Trial work was not his forte. She knew he didn't relish the idea of convincing a jury that Bobby didn't murder his wife.

CHAPTER 13

THE PROSECUTORS

Two lawyers opposing each other in a criminal trial is like two people being chased by a bear, Cary Piel says. You don't have to outrun the bear. You just have to outrun the other person.

It was a footrace in the courtroom between Cary and Susan Piel and Rick Hagen. They all ran hard. But the bear, in the end, had his meal.

In September 2008, during the week after my story ran in the *Denton Record-Chronicle*, District Attorney Paul Johnson called Cary Piel into his office. Look at the Lozano case file, Johnson said. See if it's worth pursuing.

Piel dug out the files full of documents and the boxes of evidence. He gave them to his wife, Susan. Look at this, he asked her. See if there's a case we can win. She examined the files and came back to him.

"Oh, hell yes," she said.

Piel tackled the files himself. Then he went back to the DA.

"Oh, hell yes," he told Johnson.

Though Piel was the "first chair" prosecutor for the 362nd District Court and Susan was chief misdemeanor prosecutor, they were assigned to work together on the case. It took over their work time. It took over their lives. It *was* their lives for a year.

Cary was elated to have Susan by his side on a case of this magnitude. He still had trials scheduled, but as a division chief, she didn't have a caseload of her own. So she began immediately to lay out the case and to decide which of them should do which part of the work.

"No other attorney would I have trusted to do that," Cary said. "I know what she is capable of. I knew I could trust her. I knew that I could concentrate on my part and let her do her part and it would be done well."

Susan Piel is an attractive woman with lovely eyes and an appealing figure. Cary Piel is a spark plug of a man with so much vitality that he seems to be bouncing off the walls even when he is sitting still. They'd first met in the district attorney's office as young prosecutors. Bruce Isaacks had hired Cary to prosecute family violence cases, and Susan worked in that division as well.

"We keep him in a cage," Isaacks said when he hired Cary. "We only let him out to prosecute cases."

Cary had a reputation as a street fighter, a bit of a hothead. Around Susan, he gentled. They married and had three children. When the children were young, Susan stopped working, but she later came back to the law as the children grew older. Cary also left at one point to pursue private practice, a much more lucrative way of using his law degree. But when Johnson won the election away from Isaacks, he wanted Cary and Susan both on his team, and Cary returned. Susan already was working there again after having her last baby.

Cary and Susan Piel both met with Ranger Tracy Murphree and began to go through the Lozano files word by word. They worked hours, days, weeks. They examined the photographs of the crime scene and the evidence taken piece by piece off the bed minutely—and one day, it hit them.

"The freaking shell casing was under the box," Murphree said. "There was our smoking gun. That shell casing could not have gotten under the box on its own. Someone staged that scene. We took the evidence off and moved it to the end of the bed before we logged it in the evidence log. So when we finally found the shell casing in the folds of the blanket, it just didn't occur to us that the box had been on top of it. I'd had several more years of experience by the time we were preparing for the trial. That will never happen to me again."

The crime scene team should have caught that, but they missed it because they hadn't used the proper process for logging in evidence. Because they'd moved the evidence in stages, the crime scene team had not realized that the shell casing they recovered from the blanket actually lay *under* the box of gun-cleaning equipment, *under* the newspaper. It was unfortunate that there were no police measurements to back it up, but Cary Piel compared the photographs using the tiger pattern on the blanket. He was sure he could prove to a jury that someone had to have placed the newspaper and the box atop the shell casing, after the gunshot. That shell casing, ejected from the semiautomatic pistol, had landed on the blanket. It could not have accidentally rolled under the heavy box. Viki had died instantly. She hadn't moved the shell casing under the box. Someone else had staged the scene.

The Piels made another discovery. The murder file contained a computer-generated diagram of the bed, and one detail as pictured would hurt their case. Detective Jeff Wawro had used his personal computer software to diagram the relationship of the items on the bed. The software was from his side business as a contractor, and he'd actually drawn up the plans for the Lozano house. The software didn't allow a 3-D image, however, and in the drawing he made he'd placed the casing north of the box, not underneath. The software wasn't meant for forensic work, and he'd only wanted to give detectives a picture to work from. He made it simply to give himself and the other detectives some points of reference. It wasn't meant to become evidence. But it did. He didn't imagine that it would ever be seen in court. But the Piels handed it over to Hagen in discovery, as they did everything in the file, and ultimately, it gave Hagen a springboard from which to launch his theory that police were lying about the position of the shell casing under the box. The police had no photos to back up their claims, and their own diagram seemed to show it lying to the side of the box, not under it.

That diagram would prove to be one of the toughest hurdles for the prosecution to overcome.

With the help of investigator Jack Grassman, Susan Piel began contacting witnesses and doing preliminary interviews. There were the five girlfriends who had talked to Denton police, some of them very reluctantly. To use all of them in the courtroom would seem like they were picking on the defendant, she decided. Besides, all of them were afraid, and a couple of them were so shaky they could have done more harm than good. She chose the last two. Karen Algrim and Cindy Waters were with Bobby close in time to the crime, and each had evidence that his wife's death was on his mind. He'd told Karen that Viki was dying of leukemia. He'd told Cindy that his wife likely would not live through her pregnancy and childbirth. Both stories were lies.

———————

Judge Bruce McFarling set a trial date of April 20, 2009. The Piels knew they weren't ready for that early date, and they knew that Hagen wasn't ready either. Defense lawyers usually get one free pass, when the judge accepts whatever excuse the lawyer comes up with to postpone, or continue, the trial. With a client free on bail and the possibility that he will be sentenced to prison, there is no reason a defense lawyer would want an early trial.

But Rick Hagen had a small problem. It was no secret that Hagen planned to use the argument that Bobby's right to a speedy trial had been violated because the first case had been dropped years earlier and then he was reindicted. If

Hagen wanted another continuance, he would have to argue that he needed more time while still arguing that Bobby had not been given a speedy trial. Cary Piel knew that Hagen wanted him to be the one to ask for a continuance. He didn't, even though he wanted one. He gutted it out, he said, knowing that Hagen wanted the extra time and was banking on the defense attorney's blinking first. It was a game of legal chicken.

Finally, at one of the first pretrial hearings, Hagen asked McFarling for more time to prepare his case.

Counselor, the judge said, you realize that you have two issues before the court today. One is that you need more time, and the other is that too much time has passed already. Hagen nodded.

Prosecutor Carl Piel admitted later that he too needed more time but could not be the one to ask for the continuance with the speedy trial issue on the table. The judge granted the continuance and said he would consider the speedy trial issue as testimony proceeded during the trial. While a jury was listening to the evidence to determine whether Bobby killed his wife, McFarling would also be considering that same evidence to determine whether he should rule that having two indictments seven years apart should be considered one case against Bobby and whether that violated the speedy trial act.

Hagen wanted a pretrial hearing that would have aired all the testimony of all the witnesses before the trial. That would have given him information to use in his attack on those witnesses. Cary Piel objected strenuously. McFarling settled the matter by ruling that the issue could be considered along with the trial testimony, saving weeks of time and Piel's case from premature airing.

Cary Piel was building a case using the police and Texas Rangers investigations and the medical examiner evidence. Susan Piel was in charge of the women. Not just the girlfriends, but also Viki's mother, Anna Farish—who would not be a help to the prosecution—Viki's schoolteacher colleagues and Viki's ob-gyn. The doctor was important. She would refute Bobby's claims that Viki had leukemia, or that her life was ever in peril during her pregnancy. She would tell jurors that Viki had never been too ill and weak to care for her baby and that she did indeed care for Monty herself. The doctor also remembered that Bobby's main concern about Viki's health seemed to be that his wife was gaining too much weight.

"Cary was totally building a case on his side, and I was totally building a case on my side, and it was very powerful," Susan said.

That summer they worked full time on the case. They'd sit out by their backyard pool on Sunday mornings drinking coffee and planning strategy. The case never went away. They told the nanny who looked after their three children to expect long days and extra duty. Susan usually did the shuffling of children from school to football practice to social events to home. This year, there would not be time for that until the trial was over.

They did take a week just before the trial to bring both of their sons to camps in different states, and later, two-a-days football practice began for their older son, further complicating their lives. The work was interrupted twice so one or the other could drive him to the morning and evening practices. Still, the case was always with them.

Their most productive meeting, they remember, was one Sunday morning out by the pool. Cary planned a traditional beginning to the prosecution. He would bring his law enforcement witnesses to the stand first. Susan disagreed.

Everything that law enforcement had to say had to be put into the context of what was going on in Bobby's life that pressured him into making the decisions he made, she believed. The first witnesses should be Karen and Cindy. Jurors would know from the lies he had told to the women in his life, the way he manipulated them, the lengths he would go to so he could maintain his lifestyle, what Bobby was capable of, what he was up to, before they heard what he did.

Cary was worried that the jury would spend a day and a half without ever hearing about a crime. But he gave in.

"There's not another lawyer in this office who could have changed my mind," he says. "But I trusted her. And she knew what those women had to say was going to be damning."

Besides, after a pretrial hearing on the admissibility of the women's testimony, they believed that Hagen feared what they had to say. They'd put all five women's names and the thrust of each one's testimony on a chart for the admissibility hearing. Hagen had argued hard for throwing all of it out. It was not relevant to Viki's death, he argued, and would prejudice the jury against his client. McFarling frowned at the number of women on the chart. The Piels then agreed to limit the girlfriend testimony to two women—just what they wanted in the first place.

Karen Algrim wasn't especially happy about telling her secrets on the witness stand. She had moved to a different area, married and had two children. But she was composed and ready to tell the truth.

Cindy Waters was terrified. She wavered between knowing that Bobby must have killed his wife to saying that the man she had loved just could not have done such a thing. The first time Susan Piel and her investigator, Jack Grassman, drove to meet Cindy at her home for an appointment, they arrived to find her running out the door. She was bolting. She had panicked at the last minute and decided to skip the interview. But she went back inside with them and talked for three hours. Most of the time her cockatiel was standing on her shoulder. Susan watched, mesmerized, as the bird pulled one of Cindy's earrings from her ear and walked back and forth across her chest while the former cop talked about the months, weeks and days leading up to Viki's death.

Cindy couldn't seem to separate the lies Bobby had told her from the truth of the situation. For example, she talked about the day Bobby filed for divorce, even though she had been told that had never actually happened. Her reality that final year was the reality Bobby created for her, and it had left her confused and scared.

Even as she agreed to testify against him, the Piels believed that a part of Cindy still was in love with the man she had thought Bobby was. The fantasy knight who was going to carry her away on his white horse. That was the man he had claimed to be, in the world he had created for her. It was hard, even then, to replace that world with the real one where the man she'd loved had put a bullet in his wife's chest.

Cindy told them how she and Bobby had stayed together after his wife's death, at first hiding their relationship from the world, but after the first indictment was dropped, becoming a little more public. Still, Bobby never spent a night at her house. He always went home to Anna Farish.

She told them that they had been building a house together in Krugerville, a tiny town northeast of Denton. Bobby was using the money from selling his share of the La Mancha house to his mother-in-law. But his expensive taste soon outran his budget, and they argued over the lavish additions. The excitement seemed to be leaking out of their relationship. And Cindy had a suspicion that Bobby was having an affair with his son's schoolteacher.

When they finally split up, Cindy became afraid of Bobby and moved to Tennessee. But eventually she'd come back and began anew with her former husband, the father of her two little boys.

In June 2009 Judge McFarling heard a motion from defense attorney Rick Hagen for a change of venue. Bobby and Renee, the woman he'd been seeing since before Cindy left—the one who'd been Monty's teacher—arrived early.

Bobby had a large Bible in his hands. They sat at the back of the courtroom while the judge considered other matters. They sat close together with the Bible open on their laps. With their heads close together, they discussed verses of the chapters they were reading, and Bobby marked the Bible with a yellow marking pen. As they flipped through the holy book, it was visibly marked heavily in hot pink and yellow highlighter. The newly married Lozanos, it seemed, had found religion and wanted everyone to know it.

Jarrett Whitehead, Renee's ex-husband and the father of her three children, had known her as Heidi. Until she met Bobby, Renee was an unused middle name, he said.

And that wasn't the only thing that changed when Renee and Bobby got together. Whitehead and his former wife were both hippies. "She was 'Miss Natural,'" he said. "She had long brown hair and long hair under her arms and on her legs." But after she started seeing Bobby, Renee became much slimmer. Way too thin, he thought. She became a blonde. She dressed expensively, with fashionably polished nails.

Before the divorce, she and Whitehead had lived in an apartment on the campus at Selwyn, the Montessori school where Renee taught and where Monty Lozano attended classes. Whitehead believed his wife threw him out because she became involved with one of their female neighbors; that woman threw her husband out as well, he remembered. He never had any proof of a lesbian romance, and soon Renee was involved with Bobby.

He moved back home to Georgia and was paying child

support for their three children and having a hard time financially. But just before Thanksgiving one year they began talking about reuniting. They made plans for him to drive down and spend Thanksgiving with her and the children. He was on the road to Texas when Renee called. Don't come, she said. She had met someone else and fallen in love. He wasn't welcome anymore.

Whitehead went anyway.

When he drove up, he saw a Lincoln Navigator parked outside the apartment. He saw a man walking by, with Whitehead's own youngest son on his shoulders. He saw his former wife and was struck by the changes in her look. Renee told him that if he insisted on staying with his children, she would go to her mother's. He left knowing that there would be no reconciliation.

In later years, Whitehead said he visited his children at two fancy homes where Renee and Bobby lived. One in Plano had statuary in the backyard near the pool, he said.

For a while, the couple was going to move to Mexico. Whitehead fought that. Then the plan changed. They had an opportunity to open a chain of real estate offices in Croatia. Whitehead was sick, thinking he would never see his children again, but he had no money to fight them in court. Then, suddenly the move was off.

Whitehead wasn't sure what had happened, but it seemed that Renee and Bobby had crashed financially. They were living in Denton in a house he understood belonged to Bobby's brother-in-law. His ex-wife called him one night, begging for money. "She said if I didn't wire her five hundred dollars the electricity would be turned off the next day. I couldn't let my children live that way. I sent the money."

Apparently finances didn't improve, and Whitehead learned that they were all moving in with Anna Farish, Bobby's former mother-in-law. He was flabbergasted. From his children he learned that the three younger children, Bobby's son and Whitehead's two younger children, all shared one bedroom, and his older daughter, a teenager, had moved into what was formerly an in-house theater. You had to walk through the sunken bar and the poolroom to reach her bedroom, Whitehead learned when he went to the house one day to pick up the children. Heidi Renee bragged that they had big plans to enlarge the house. They would add a second story, she said.

"They claimed to have jobs, but I don't see how," Whitehead said. "They said they wrote contracts for houses." But the truth, most likely, came from the children. "My youngest son told me that Grandma Farish is their money tree."

Renee and Bobby Lozano had begun a real estate business, Exclusively Lozano, together. The website showed Renee as a silvery blonde, posed provocatively near the house they were showcasing. One photo showed her bending over Bobby's back with her backside in the air and her long blond hair streaming down her back.

Now in court, however, the new Mrs. Lozano had changed her look drastically. Her hair was a much shorter cut and had been dyed a mousy brown. Sometimes she affected reading glasses; sometimes not. Chances were that Hagen knew that his client would be portrayed as a womanizer who preferred blondes. With Bobby's new wife's hair as a not-so-subtle contrast, Hagen likely hoped to dispel that vision.

Hagen argued hard for a change of venue. The *Denton Record-Chronicle*'s September 7, 2008, investigative story outlined the whole case, Hagen argued. Subsequent stories pointed out that Bobby was indicted only three weeks later, he said. The newspaper had convicted Bobby in the public eye and was bragging about its influence, and that influence went against his client. That presented too much pretrial publicity for Bobby to have a fair trial in Denton County. Hagen called *Record-Chronicle* managing editor Dawn Cobb to the stand to give circulation figures for the newspaper. Though its regular newspaper circulation is mostly on the north end of the county, its online circulation was throughout the county and much higher, Hagen argued.

Cary Piel questioned Cobb too and then argued that the online circulation included the entire Dallas County and Tarrant County areas of Dallas and Fort Worth, and those readers were not eligible Denton County jurors.

Hagen pointed out that he had been contacted by producers from *48 Hours*, *Dateline* and *20/20* television crime shows. The trial was destined to generate much more publicity before it even began, he said. He wanted the trial to be moved to Austin, where he could use a law school courtroom so district courts would not be interrupted.

Piel argued the extreme cost to the county of housing 150 witnesses and court personnel.

The judge told the lawyers he would not move the trial.

But if the jury selection process proved difficult because too many people had formed an opinion about the case, then he would take the question up again, he said.

During voir dire, the lawyers learned that few prospective jurors had even heard of Bobby Lozano.

The Piels hired a local forensic expert to go through the evidence. They had to supply his name to Rick Hagen, and at some point Cary Piel figured out that Hagen was building his defense against testimony he assumed the expert would give. Piel didn't have to tell Hagen everything, and he never told him that they decided not to use the expert at all. He later believed that decision may have thrown Hagen off stride. He was waiting to unleash his strategy on a witness who never appeared.

The Piels complemented each other in the courtroom. Susan was pretty, likable, intelligent and calm. Cary was unpredictable. He used sarcasm like a surgical scalpel. He was witty and personable—at least, when he wanted to be.

Against the Piels, Rick Hagen came off as pedantic. His voice in questioning the prosecution witnesses was often a monotone. He couldn't afford to be genial with the police witnesses. He seemed surly. Still, he was very smart, and he'd pulled off surprise wins before.

Was he fast enough to outrun the bear?

CHAPTER 14

THE TRIAL BEGINS

Potential jurors milled around the second floor of the courthouse on Tuesday morning, July 21, 2009—bored, tired, waiting for their turn at a short personal interview with the lawyers. There were a few seats in a couple of alcoves, but nowhere near enough for everyone. They'd spent the whole of Monday in voir dire, and they were ready to either be picked or to go home or back to work.

Occasionally the bailiff would call a name and that juror would go inside the large "ceremonial" courtroom where jury selection was taking place. The rest leaned against walls, peered over the railing at the first floor below, hoarded the few chairs or sat on the floor. Finally, one of the lawyers realized their discomfort. The bailiff led them into the central jury room, where there were vending machines and at least enough chairs for everyone to sit.

The relief did not extend to me.

As the morning dragged on, I leaned against a pillar for a while, resting first one high-heeled foot and then the other. I moved to lean against a wall, and finally a spot opened up on a bench down the hall. I could still see if they were all called back into the courtroom, and I could see if they were dismissed for lunch. It was better than standing, my feet told me. A very large woman in a blue dress limped over and sat next to me. The bench cracked and groaned. I feared it would break. But it held, creaking every time she moved. I tried to read the book I had brought, keeping an eye on the lady for any quick moves that might bring us down, bench and all.

I had kept a check on the voir dire the entire previous day too, but I had suspected that it would go on for more than a single day. I had been right. And now I could not leave for fear of missing something.

At last, the bailiff told the sixty-six people to go to lunch and to return at 2:30 P.M. When court resumed, it was in Judge Bruce McFarling's own courtroom on the third floor of the courthouse. It was much smaller and couldn't hold nearly as many spectators. But it adjoined the judge's chambers and was his own territory. This is where the case would be heard. Trials are not set up for the comfort and pleasure of spectators.

McFarling had been young for a judge when he ran for office ten years earlier. He had affected suspenders and conservative clothing since taking the bench. I thought he might be trying to look more the part of the wise judge. Now, with white around the edges of his dark hair and a more middle-aged span to his girth, he didn't need to work to look older. But he still wore suspenders and dark suits under his judge's robe. He had regularly played dominoes with Judge Phillip Vick during the lunch period in years past when he was a young prosecutor. When Vick retired, the domino game moved to McFarling's court. He was a genial judge who never became ill-tempered with lawyers trying their tricks. He quietly made his decisions on objections and kept the momentum of the trial moving along. As a reporter who has seen courtroom meltdowns and long delays, I appreciated that.

When McFarling summoned the jury pool back into the courtroom, he called thirteen names. The jury consisted of eleven women and two men. One of the women was an alternate who would sit in the trial and not deliberate but would be ready just in case one of the other jurors could not continue. Most of the female jurors were young. One was Hispanic. Would that help or hurt Bobby, I wondered? Would he woo them with his eyes and charm them with his smile? Would they listen to his lies and hate him for the lothario he was portrayed to be? It was an interesting jury.

I quickly found a place in the second row of the "groom's side" of the courtroom, which was what prosecutors called the section behind the defense table. The term had no religious significance. They just considered themselves the most important part of the proceding. I was directly behind Renee Lozano. I sensed that she didn't want me there, but it was a prime spot for seeing both the witness stand and the jurors' faces. I stuck there for most of the trial until Lozano relatives eventually over-filled the first row and took my spot. I never tried to sit there after that. I knew the family was angry with me, and it made me a bit uncomfortable. But at least they were civil, and I smiled at them as though they didn't hate me. It really wasn't their fault that Bobby had murdered his wife, I thought.

Renee Lozano came into the courtroom carrying the big Bible that had been a prop for her and Bobby during all the pretrial sessions. Her drab brown dyed hair was pulled down in a low ponytail at the base of her neck with a sparkly clip. She wore an expensive-looking suit with a green jacket and a short, tight black skirt. When she sat, she covered the exposed expanse of leg with a black wool afghan.

Bobby's sister, Blanca, sat next to her. She and her husband, David White, had flown in from Mexico for the trial. White had been the first judge of the 362nd District Court, where he now sat in support of the defendant in a murder trial. He had retired from the bench and married Blanca, who'd worked as a translator at the courthouse, and they had moved to Mexico several years earlier. White had been friendly to me when he was a judge. Now, he nodded at me and occasionally spoke. He wore suits every day to the courthouse. Blanca wore expensive-looking clothing that clearly came from Mexico. She looked good in it. Her dark hair was styled in a short spike that should have looked too young for her but somehow suited her face perfectly.

Later, Bobby's older brother Frank came to the courtroom to join Blanca and David White in the front row with Renee.

Bobby sat in front of the bar, impeccably dressed as usual, in a suit that fit him perfectly, as though it had not been pulled off a rack but made for him. He didn't look at his wife much during the trial, but she never seemed to take her eyes off him.

I would come to wonder, during moments of testimony that revealed Bobby's obvious lies and his complicity, just what Renee was thinking. I sat behind her and couldn't see most of her expressions. Later, looking at photos of her face during testimony, I had a good idea. The photos, taken from the front corner of the courtroom, often revealed shock, anger and grief. I wondered what their evenings at home were like after they put all the children to bed.

People who'd known Viki said that Renee looked just like her. There was certainly a resemblance; when she was blond, Renee looked like Viki had at her death, with long honey-colored hair hanging down her back. Even after she became a brunette, Renee looked like Viki's yearbook photo, when her hair had been just above shoulder length and darker.

It seemed clear to me that Bobby had a vision of the ideal woman. He worked on each of the women in his life, making them thin and blond and shiny with a facade of wealth and good upkeep. I wondered what that "ideal" meant, especially coming from a Hispanic man from a working-class family background. Bobby only ever seemed to have been interested in Caucasian women.

Anna Farish never came to the courthouse unless she was on the stand. Presumably, Bobby did not want her to hear any damning testimony. Besides, he and Renee needed her support, both emotionally and financially. She only showed up to testify in Bobby's defense, and then someone took her home. Anna Farish still believed in the reality that her son-in-law had created for her.

CHAPTER 15

OPENING STATEMENTS

The courtroom filled almost immediately. Misdemeanor prosecutors crowded together on the back rows, bringing along file folders to appear busy as they watched their boss, Susan Piel, working at the prosecutors' table in front of the bar. Several other courthouse employees drifted in and sat near the back, AWOL from their duties at desks in several offices. The general public ventured timidly in. Most had never watched a trial before. Soon, there were no seats left. A few dragged in chairs from the anteroom in front of the court, and some stood. When Judge McFarling arrived, he frowned at the bailiff, who told those without a regular seat they had to leave. There would be no standing in the courtroom during the trial. All the rolling chairs were pulled out of the small conference room between the courtroom and the hallway, but they were later returned one by one as law enforcement officers showed up and were granted a place to sit.

It was time for the formal reading of the indictment. Bobby Lozano and his defense attorney, Rick Hagen, stood, and Hagen put his arm around his client.

"How do you plead?" the judge asked after reading the formal words.

"Ladies and gentlemen, I am not guilty," Bobby replied.

Cary Piel stood for his opening statement and got right down to it. Bobby had killed his wife Viki in her "faded blue jammies with duckies on them," Piel said. He'd killed her in a state of anger and confliction and shot her "BOOM!" in the heart.

"Evidence will show he was thinking of it for some time," Piel stated. "But that he didn't plan on shooting her that night."

Viki had been eating popcorn in bed when she was shot. Piel said Bobby cleaned up the scene and moved the popcorn bowl out of the room. He picked up stray popcorn pieces but didn't get them all. Some remained in the bed. Some were down the front of Viki's loose pajama shirt. One small piece remained in her mouth, and a lot of it was undigested in her stomach. Then Bobby staged the scene to look like a gun-cleaning accident, Piel told the jury. He pulled back the covers, causing a mirror-image bloodstain on the top covers, and put a newspaper on top of them near Viki's hand. He sprayed the Glock with gun oil—much too much gun oil—and it dripped onto the newspaper. He laid out the cleaning kit and put a cloth in the cleaning tool. But in his haste, Bobby could not find the shell casing. When he shot her, it had ejected from the Glock and landed in a fold of the covers. He'd then put the newspaper and cleaning kit on top of it. This was a damning piece of evidence, Piel said.

"Then he goes to the tanning salon so he can come in and say, 'Oh, this is what I found.'"

Piel didn't mention that, if Viki was dead when Bobby left, as the prosecution believed, that meant that Bobby left his son alone in the house with no one to care for him. The baby would have been alone with only his dead mother for company.

Jurors watched Piel as he moved around the space in front of them. He was animated, waving his arms as expressions ranging from anger to mockery flitted across his face. He told the jury about one of Bobby's two girlfriends he planned to put on the witness stand. She'd been young, he said, an intern in the social work program. Unmarried and a bit naive. Bobby's wife and mother-in-law apparently believed the lies he told to get out of the house to visit her.

"He tells his family he's some kind of ninja warrior and he's got to go out and save the world every Friday night," Piel said.

The other girlfriend had been another detective at the police department. This was not a casual affair, the prosecutor said. Bobby Lozano hadn't wanted to lose her. He'd promised her marriage. He'd promised her he would leave his wife, but he missed deadlines for moving out, and Cindy Waters got tired of waiting. After she learned that he lied about going with his wife on a trip instead of spending the weekend with her, she told him it was over. Bobby didn't want that, but he couldn't risk losing his wife's money.

"Here was a guy who is a snazzy dresser. He's too sexy for his shirts," Piel said. "This is a guy who takes a change of clothes to double-header softball games."

Bobby Lozano had a $300,000 life insurance policy on his wife. A few months before her death, he talked her into another policy, for a million dollars. The Piels had learned that the smaller insurance policy had eventually gone to Monty after the company sued Bobby to keep from having to pay. But the larger policy had paid without question.

Piel told the jury he would show them a lease Bobby signed for an apartment he never set foot into. He'd needed to convince Cindy that he really was going to leave his wife, though he wasn't. He told them that Cindy would testify to a strange meeting she had with Bobby a few days before the murder, when he'd asked her to meet him in a parking lot and then gave her back all the letters she had written him and he had been keeping in his desk at work. His explanation? He said he'd slapped Viki for the first time ever and she was going to press charges and the letters would look bad when his desk was searched.

Piel said he would show them the statement Bobby wrote, describing his wonderful, "magic" marriage and the tragic death of his beloved wife.

"It was a very detailed statement," Piel said. "It was a piece of work."

Rick Hagen took over the podium. He didn't move

around much, and his speech was slow, steady and ponderous. Seven years ago, a board-certified pathologist said the manner of Viki's death was "undetermined," Hagen said. Five years ago, another board-certified pathologist said it was a suicide.

"You cannot tell whether it was suicide, homicide or an accident," Hagen said.

Viki and her mother both knew that Bobby was unfaithful, he told the jury. But Viki loved Bobby anyway. Their anniversary evening out gave her hope. They spoke of their wonderful baby son, and she dreamed of having a good marriage again. But that didn't last long.

"Her hopes were destroyed. He told her he had to go to the office, and she knew what that meant. She knew that's not what he was going to do."

Hagen went on with his speech, telling jurors that Cindy Waters fell in love with Bobby and put pressure on him to leave his wife. Bobby wanted them both, Hagen said, sounding oddly like a prosecutor instead of a defense lawyer. But that would be the basis for his argument that Viki committed suicide—the left prong of his defense. The right prong was that it was an accidental discharge, an idea backed at first by Viki's mother, Anna. Hagen chose neither. He straddled the line, hoping the jurors would choose one or the other—anything but murder.

"Viki told Anna they were going to the shooting range and taking the baby," he said. "Viki cleaning that gun was nothing new. Anna had seen her cleaning the gun on the bed before."

Hagen began his case for sloppy police work with his

opening statement, a case he would repeat with every law enforcement witness. He cited reports that differed in stating whether one or both of Viki's legs were hanging off the bed. He said he would prove that the dogs were on the bed "licking blood off the body" when officers arrived. He cited Viki's unexplained bruises, which he said came from her having fired the gun herself.

Bobby Lozano's Glock service pistol was one of the "most dangerous weapons in the world," Hagen said, drawing sharp looks from people in the courtroom who owned them and deemed them to be very safe. "It's an assault weapon. A combat weapon. There is no external safety—only a little tiny safety on the trigger."

The case was dead, the indictment dismissed, until a newspaper article caused a stir and the new district attorney took it to a grand jury eighteen days later with no new evidence, Hagen said. But the state's own photographs would show that all was not as it seemed, he said. "The eye of the tiger" would prove his client's innocence, he said dramatically.

"Stay tuned for defense exhibit number ten."

At 9 A.M. Wednesday, Karen Algrim took the stand as the first state's witness. She was a pretty blonde, obviously quite a bit younger than Bobby. She didn't look at him but smiled at prosecutor Susan Piel as Piel led her through the first getting-to-know-you questions to settle her nerves. Algrim said she had lived in Denton in the late 1990s while she attended the University of North Texas. She had had an internship at the police department and worked with police social worker Richard Godoy. Bobby seemed to always be around, flirting and flattering. When he asked her out initially, she'd said no. Undeterred, he asked her again and again. Godoy warned her about Bobby's reputation, Algrim said, but finally she gave in. They started seeing each other in early 2000. They'd had a schedule, she said. He visited her every Tuesday night. On Fridays, he spent the night at her place. She told the jury that Bobby told his wife he was doing surveillance work for a covert agency, maybe the DEA, she thought.

He told Karen Algrim that he didn't love his wife and that she called him "cold," she testified. Bobby said Viki's family had money. He drove a BMW and dressed much better than the other officers Algrim saw at the police department. He said he had a million-dollar life insurance policy out on his wife, and he told her that Viki's father had set up a trust fund for him before he died that would begin soon, and he could leave his wife after that.

Algrim said she'd considered them a couple.

"My expectations were that we were going to be married," she said. "He had given me a promise ring." She met Blanca, Bobby's sister. Bobby took Algrim to baseball games and did not seem to care that his coworkers saw them together.

"It was public and awkward," she said.

In 2001, he told Algrim that Viki had leukemia and only six months to live.

"He would cry about it. He would say it should have been him, not her. He talked about putting her out of her pain," the young woman testified. "He said he poisoned a couple of dogs to see how they reacted to it but they suffered horribly so he decided not to do it."

By the time she was ready to graduate from the university, Karen Algrim realized that Bobby was not going to leave his wife, no matter how many impassioned declarations of love he made. And he was jealous of her male friends and was possessive. He didn't want her to go out when he was not around. She moved away at the end of the school year, leaving him behind.

Defense attorney Rick Hagen cross-examined Karen Algrim carefully. She knew Bobby was married? Yes. She believed that she had changed him and that he loved her? Yes. She became a little frustrated because he didn't leave his wife? No. She didn't get that frustrated, she told the defense attorney.

"At the beginning, he told me that he cheated on his wife the day before his marriage and the day after," Algrim told Susan Piel in redirect questioning.

"And how did he seem with that?"

"Cocky," she said.

———————

Former Denton police detective Cindy Waters was the next witness. As she entered the courtroom, Cindy was wider of hip than in her days with Bobby, but she was lovely. Her blond hair was piled artfully on her head and fell softly around her eyes. She spoke in a soft, firm voice and didn't pull any punches about her role in Bobby's life or marriage. Susan Piel read letter after sugary letter, causing one man in the gallery to say during a break that he "wanted to puke." Letters written after Monty was born described in glowing terms their future life together with Bobby as the daddy and Cindy as the mommy of her two little boys and Monty. Cindy opened one envelope and brushed at her lap as dried rose petals fell from the pages.

'Sin,'

How sensuous the name as it drips from my mouth. How passionate the possessor of this name does love me. The twinkle in your eyes, the same born of an unsuspected moment long ago, does still enchant our loving gazes.

The purple passage continued in the short love letter. He wrote that he "breathed" her even when she was not there. He cherished her embrace and the warmth of her smile, he wrote. He longed to be near her. He told her to close her eyes and sense his lips hovering over hers.

Breathe slowly, deeply, rhythmically as only we can imagine the passion swirling between them. As in the beginning, so shall it be in the end.

All my love,
Roberto

"He was a very giving person," Cindy said. "He was very attentive to my emotions. He was polished. But he expected you to take care of yourself and always look nice. I lost forty pounds. It was very important to him."

Cindy said that she and her ex-husband had been having problems even before she became pregnant with their second son, long before she started seeing Bobby. They had discussed divorce, but when they learned they were going to have a baby, they remained together and tried to make the marriage work after the baby was born. But it wasn't working. They sold their house and split their property but remained together in a rented house because they couldn't afford to live separately. They both knew it was over, but they were living together nonetheless.

Then Bobby came into the picture.

Cindy had gained weight during her last pregnancy, and she wanted to look better. Bobby offered to work out with her and help her with a diet. She knew he was married too, but soon they were sexually involved.

"He told me there was not very much of a sexual relationship between [him and Viki]. He told me they had mutually decided there would be a divorce," Cindy testified.

But then in February 2001, he told her that his wife of fifteen years was pregnant. He couldn't leave her yet. Cindy understood. She was willing to wait. He would stay for a period after the baby was born and then they would be free to marry, he told her. Cindy went ahead with her own divorce. Later, Cindy learned that Bobby had known of Viki's pregnancy much earlier, at Christmas in fact.

They met at Bobby's sister Blanca's apartment. Blanca was single at the time and allowed her brother to bring Cindy there for trysts.

Issues, issues, issues
   I humorously admit that we have a few. And yet, my love, it serves only to draw me closer to you.

In this letter Bobby wrote that he had never felt so transparent with another person. Though they had yet to share unbridled passion, he wrote,

   . . . we remain irreversibly enchanted with expectation. Torturous, awe-inspiring expectation.

Susan Piel handed Cindy a stack of letters, the ones Bobby had given back to her when he said he was going to be investigated for slapping his wife. The stack also contained several letters Bobby had written to her, and Susan had them blown up in large print so the jury could read them. She asked Cindy to follow along on the originals as she read them aloud. Occasionally, she would ask Cindy the meaning of some flowery phrase.

Bobby and Cindy had talked often on a pair of cell phones he bought them together on a family plan. Even more often, they paged each other with a code. "1,2,3,4" meant, "I love you and I'm thinking about you." Jurors blinked. He had used the same code with Karen.

He visited Cindy the day his son was born. Later he

brought the baby to Blanca's apartment so Cindy could hold him. He took several months off from work for paternity leave.

On February 12, 2002, the anniversary of their first sexual encounter, he sent her a printed "to my wife on our anniversary" card. Soon after Monty was born, Bobby wanted to have a professional photograph taken with the two of them, her two boys and the baby.

"I said no."

Bobby told Cindy in April that he and Viki had seen a lawyer and agreed on a settlement. Later, he said they'd filed the divorce documents. Suspicious, Cindy looked for the divorce listed in public documents, but she couldn't find any trace. Bobby explained it away by telling her that Anna was embarrassed and had paid an extra ten thousand dollars to have the records sealed.

In June there came a series of delays in the separation. He planned to tell his parents, but family came into town to visit and it wasn't a good time. Then he said he told them, asking to live with them for a few months, and his mother refused. His mother told him to stay with his wife, Bobby told Cindy. He was very sad, she recalled, but vowed he would rent an apartment.

Another deadline passed, and he said he couldn't leave because Viki was unstable. She was trying to poison him and the baby, Bobby said. He had to stay to protect Monty. Cindy then told the jury about the weekend when they were supposed to be together and he said he had to take his father to Mexico for a family emergency. But when she drove by his father's house, the elder Lozano was out mowing his lawn. Cindy cried when she said she knew it was time to give up. Bobby was never leaving his wife, just as her friends had warned her.

It was Bobby who seemed unstable, she testified. Cindy told her friend Jackie that she feared for herself and for Viki. Still, they worked together at the police department. Bobby made a pretext on Friday, July 5, to take her to help him make an arrest. Instead he took her to lunch and begged her to be patient. He wanted to go back to her place and have sex. She said no.

And now I face this life without you. By choice, your choice, never by design. As I have last declared in my previous letter, you must follow your heart. Love should never be a torturous affair. It bears ecstasy. Redemption. A soliloquy of incomparable exuberance. A hierarchy of gentle, passionate grace. Please, have this last message forever emblazoned in your memory.

I love you. Today, tomorrow and forever.
Roberto

He called her about 11 P.M. on July 5, his sixteenth anniversary, and when Cindy stepped out on the porch to smoke a cigarette while she talked on the phone, she found Bobby standing outside her door. Once again he promised everything would be as they planned, she said. He said he would ride up on a white horse, which would be a moving van, and carry her away. He said the divorce was still on. They made love.

Defense attorney Rick Hagen took over questioning. Cindy had given police three written statements. What about her statement during an internal affairs interview at the police department? he asked. Susan Piel objected. That is not subject to open record, she said. Hagen insisted. Piel said she did not have that document because police won't release their internal affairs documents when no disciplinary action is involved. In this case, Cindy had resigned before the investigation was completed.

Hagen was determined. "I asked for a statement from this witness. I'm entitled to it," he insisted.

The judge sent the jury out for a break while the lawyers argued. Hagen said he would get a subpoena and have it served on the police immediately. Cary Piel argued that it was 4 P.M. and they needed to work for another hour that day. Hagen didn't want to move an inch farther without the statement, but Judge McFarling told him he either could proceed without the statement or they would bring another witness to the stand. The trial was not going to go idle for an hour, the judge said.

"My order is that you will continue on with your cross-examination," McFarling said. "When the records get here, I'll allow you time to review them."

"My point is, Judge, I don't want to start cross without seeing the statement," Hagen retorted.

"OK then, we'll move on to the next witness," McFarling said.

That next witness was fire captain Luke Scholl, resplendent in his dress uniform with gold braid and badge. He was tall, boyishly handsome, with an open, honest face. He walked with an air of confidence, and he was well-spoken. He seemed a perfect witness for a jury that consisted mostly of young women. It took only four minutes from the 911 call for the engine and ambulance to arrive at the house on La Mancha, Scholl testified. Fire Station Six was near the Montecito Del Sur subdivision. He climbed down off the quint, an engine that performs four other functions as well as pumping water, and saw a man holding a baby standing at the front door.

The dispatcher had relayed the message while they were en route that they were heading for a gunshot victim and that CPR was in progress. Usually when they arrived under those circumstances, they would hear a shout from the room where someone was desperately compressing a chest and blowing into a mouth, he testified. Not here. On that night, the man led them to a master suite where the victim lay on a bed.

There were no signs that CPR had taken place. Firstly, once the lifesaving measure had been started, it could not be stopped until paramedics arrived to take over, Scholl said. A police officer, like Bobby Lozano, was trained in CPR and would know that. Secondly, the man had no signs of blood on him. The bullet wound was exactly in the spot where the hands should be placed during CPR. Blood would have spurted out during chest compressions. There was little blood on the front of the victim's pajama top and none whatsoever on the man or the baby he was holding. You have to compress the chest hard for CPR—a third to half the depth of the chest. It caused bruises and can break ribs if done correctly. The body showed no sign of this. The man was not sweating, not out of breath. He was calm. He was standing over his wife's bloody body holding their child. One of the paramedics tried to take the baby from him, but when he started crying, the man took him back. They then asked him to leave the room, the paramedic captain testified.

The woman on the bed was cold, with a waxy, pale complexion. She had lividity up to her ankle in the leg that had fallen off the bed. Lividity starts a minimum of forty-five minutes after the heart stops beating, Scholl said.

"This obviously was not a salvageable patient," he said. "She had been dead at least an hour and very possibly a lot longer than that."

Another paramedic lifted one of the victim's shoulders and moved her loose pajama blouse aside to check for lividity in the woman's back. It was there. The paramedic laid her shoulder back on the bed, not disturbing the scene, and they left the room. Scholl said he stood by the door until a police officer took over that duty. He saw no dogs, he testified.

Hagen began his cross-examination. Would Scholl disagree with a trained pathologist that lividity could begin as early as twenty-five minutes? Scholl said he would have to disagree with that. Could he think of a reason why another paramedic would say both of the victim's legs were hanging off the bed? If anyone claimed both legs were hanging off the bed, Scholl said, they would be wrong.

Scholl left the stand, and Hagen approached the bench with a man who had just walked into the courtroom holding a document. He was an attorney for the city of Denton. He had received the subpoena but had not complied. He told the judge that city policy mandated that nothing from an internal affairs investigation could be released unless there was a sustained complaint and punishment issued. Cindy Waters had resigned before the investigation was finished; therefore, he could not release her statement.

Nevertheless, Judge McFarling ordered that the city release the statement to Hagen and also give the Piels a copy. The statement would be sealed and placed in the court's file in case there was an appeal, the judge said. The city lawyer reluctantly agreed.

Hagen won that round, but no one knew what he would actually find in the statement that Cindy had not already blurted out.

———————

The next day, Thursday, July 23, 2009, Cindy Waters was back on the witness stand, looking tense as she faced the formidable defense attorney. In answer to his questions, she said she began in police work in Sanger, a small town just north of Denton. She worked there for two years and then moved to the larger department in Denton that offered better pay.

Rick Hagen sat at his table, reading his questions from his computer screen. He showed no reaction to her answers and hardly seemed to listen to them.

You knew Bobby had a reputation as a ladies' man? Yes. A Don Juan? Yes. Friends tried to warn you that he would never leave his wife? Yes, she said. Bobby said that you changed him and that you were unlike all the rest? Yes, sir.

Hagen never referred to the statement he had demanded from the city the day before. Apparently, it had not given him any ammunition for cross-examination.

About the year and a half they spent together after his wife died: "Bobby gave you money?"

"We shared an account."

"You had trouble controlling Monty."

No real answer.

"Bobby left you."

"That's not the way it was!" she responded tearfully.

"Bobby wound up marrying Renee."

"I don't know who she is."

"Bobby wound up marrying Monty's teacher."

It was more a statement than a question. Hagen was testifying, but the prosecution didn't object.

Prosecutor Susan Piel took over questioning on redirect. Cindy told her and the jury that after she and Bobby both resigned from the police department, she had believed that Bobby was not involved in Viki's death. Bobby had asked her to talk to Hagen, his lawyer, and she had. Hagen told her that Viki's mother had visited the Denton police, and they had not given her anything to make her believe her son-in-law was involved in his wife's death. When she left the lawyer's office, Cindy testified, she was convinced that Viki had committed suicide after finding out that her husband was having another affair.

"He made me feel a lot better," she said, referring to the defense attorney. "I felt a lot of guilt that she had found out about us and that is the reason she did that."

CHAPTER 16

TESTIMONY FROM FIRST RESPONDERS

Paramedic Brandon Galbraith walked into the courtroom carrying a CPR dummy. Judge McFarling asked him to walk up to the bench and place one hand in the air and the other on the Bible. He looked at the paramedic awkwardly juggling the dummy.

"Just put him down there," the judge said, smiling.

Galbraith complied and took the oath. He testified that Bobby met the paramedics at the door when they pulled up in the ambulance. He'd seemed calm and didn't appear winded as though he'd been performing CPR, which was taxing when done right.

"I asked him, 'Have you done CPR?' He didn't answer me. He just said, 'She's in there.'"

Galbraith testified that he was the paramedic who'd lifted one of the victim's shoulders to check for lividity. It was protocol, and he had to put it in his report, he said. He saw lividity on her back. When you see that, you know the blood has not moved for a long time, he testified. He then peeled his glove back and used the back of his hand to check her skin. Cold.

"She had been dead, dead, longer than an hour," he testified.

Paramedic Jay Medford wrote in his report that Galbraith had "rolled" Viki's body, defense attorney Rick Hagen said when he took over examination.

"That's way out of line," Galbraith said, but he was stoic and unemotional in his delivery.

The paramedic tried to talk about the gunshot wound. He called the hole in her chest an "exit" wound and was corrected.

"When I look there," he said, pointing at Viki's chest on the large photograph of the death scene, "I'm calling that an exit. I'm not a cop. I don't know entrance wounds from exit wounds. I know about CPR and putting out fires."

At prosecutor Cary Piel's direction, Galbraith put the CPR dummy on the floor and demonstrated to the jurors the correct way to perform the lifesaving measure. Both his hands covered the spot in the middle of the chest where Viki's bullet wound was shown to be located. It was obvious that if Bobby had performed the procedure as he claimed, he had to have also washed his hands before paramedics arrived. But there was no time for that, judging by the 911 tape. And by timing the pause in his discussion with the dispatcher on the 911 tape, at best he could only have done CPR for twenty-five seconds anyway.

Richard Godoy was a police social worker, he testified when he took the stand. His job was to counsel victims and their families when any kind of police activity was involved. On the night of July 6, 2002, he had been paged to the Lozano house soon after the 911 call went out. He and Bobby were friends, though he hadn't approved of Bobby's womanizing, he said. Still, they socialized, and Godoy had been in the Lozano home several times.

"He was best man at my wedding," Godoy said.

"And did you work out together?" Cary Piel asked, referring to Lozano's penchant for lifting weights.

"Did it work out? Uh, no," Godoy said. "We got a divorce."

The courtroom crammed with spectators burst into laughter. Even the judge was wiping tears of laughter from his eyes. Cary Piel, too tickled to continue with that line of questioning, moved on.

What was Bobby like? Piel asked. Bobby always had his eyebrows waxed and not a hair out of place, the social worker said. He was obsessed with neatness, with looking good. What about his office at work? Any pictures of his wife? No, no pictures of Viki, Godoy said. Bobby decorated his office with really expensive photographs of wolves.

Godoy testified that the first thing he saw when he stepped inside the house the night Viki died was a cleaning bucket filled with "reddish" water. It was in the foyer, he said.

Godoy was not the only person to write in a report about the cleaning bucket and the strange water, but apparently no one ever tested the water or did anything other than comment on it. Godoy said his friend looked perfectly put together as always.

"Like he was going to take a picture for *GQ* magazine," was his testimony. Godoy said he watched Lozano as he told and retold his story of only being gone for half an hour to relatives as they arrived that night. Bobby's face would contort into "crying" expressions, but he wasn't really crying, Godoy said.

Bobby was going through the motions, but he couldn't squeeze out any tears.

His brothers cried. Frank, a University of North Texas police officer, was devastated that night. He cried along with his wife, Tricia, and she tried to tend to the baby when Monty awoke and started fussing in his crib on the opposite side of the house from the master bedroom where his mother lay.

Godoy said Bobby's other brother present that night, Javier, appeared to be in shock. "He was whispering, 'this isn't true,'" Godoy said.

Viki's brother, David, arrived shortly before their mother, Anna Farish, pulled into the driveway. Godoy said he and Lieutenant Lee Howell met her at her car and Godoy escorted her into the house.

"She was saying, 'Not my Viki. Oh no, not my Viki,'" Godoy testified.

Bobby apologized to her. She was so distraught she seemed not to notice.

Anna appeared to be nauseated. She began heaving. Godoy said he brought her a bowl and asked another officer to call 911 and have paramedics come back to the house to check her out. Godoy thought it would be a good idea for them to check Bobby's vital signs while they were at it. Bobby, he said, was still grimacing, but no tears were visible. He didn't want the paramedics to touch him, but Godoy insisted. They said he was fine.

Godoy testified that Bobby next came up to him and asked for advice. Viki wanted to be cremated, he said. How could he get that done?

"She was still in the house and he was talking about having her cremated," Godoy said. "I was just amazed."

Bobby wanted to see Viki when the medical examiner started to wheel the gurney away. They agreed that he could see her but not touch her. Godoy recalled for the jury the moment when he and Parkey stood with Bobby on the front porch as the plastic shroud was unzipped around her face. He told jurors of his shock and confusion when Bobby told her to "take care" and walked back into the house.

"It struck me as odd. I've been going to death scenes for thirteen years. I've seen a lot of people react in a lot of different ways. But never like that."

Hagen took over in cross-examination. Godoy knew, did he not, that Bobby had a history of affairs? Godoy acknowledged that. Did Bobby ever ask him to send him a page so he could get out of the house? Godoy said no.

Wasn't it true that police officers are exposed to tragedies all the time? Are they not trained to keep clear heads? Godoy acknowledged that was so. His cross-examination was brief, and he soon left the witness stand.

———

Denton County sheriff Benny Parkey was next to testify. He looked distinguished with his white mustache and salt-and-pepper hair. He wore a white shirt with his dark suit and a Texas motif tie. He had been a Denton police detective when he ran for the office of sheriff a few years earlier. He had been Bobby's partner for a while in a special career criminal unit.

"I worked a lot of cases and arrested a lot of people," he acknowledged in answer to one of Cary Piel's questions.

He described Bobby Lozano as an extremely good police officer. He was conscientious about his physical appearance, and his work space was always orderly, the sheriff recalled.

"I remember once we were chasing a criminal and we ran through a muddy field. I was kidding him about ruining his four-hundred-dollar Italian loafers," Parkey said.

What was Bobby Lozano's opinion of himself? Cary Piel wanted to know.

"He was a ten."

Parkey had been called to come to the house the night Viki died because officers thought Bobby Lozano would want support, and Parkey had been a friend. But Bobby avoided him, Parkey testified. He wouldn't talk to him. It seemed strange. Parkey was on the porch when they rolled the gurney out and unzipped the plastic body bag.

People usually get quite upset at this point and don't want to let go. That's the last time they'll ever see their loved ones at home again. Bobby's shoulders were heaving like he was sobbing, but Parkey noted that there weren't any tears. It seemed incongruous.

"I've seen a lot of different reactions, but that one seemed out of place," he said.

Cary Piel wanted to talk about the notion of cleaning a gun. Parkey said that cleaning must be done after a gun is fired, because otherwise the combination of burned and unburned powder left in the mechanism would cause a gummy mess, and the gun wouldn't fire properly if it was not removed. Given Bobby's penchant for perfection, Parkey said he couldn't imagine his former partner not cleaning his gun as soon as he returned from the firing range. The gun should have already been clean that night.

And the idea of cleaning a gun on a bed?

"I'm not allowed to clean guns on the furniture," Parkey said. "That would get me expelled from the house."

In cross-examination, Hagen asked Parkey about the part of his report that referred to Bobby as "sobbing." He was going through the motions and making the noise, Parkey said, but he was not shedding tears. And at the funeral, Bobby avoided him again.

"I was standing right there, and he didn't make eye contact with me and walked right on by."

CHAPTER 17

MORE POLICE TESTIMONY

Denton County chief deputy sheriff Lee Howell had risen through the ranks in his career at the Denton Police Department. He had been commander of the SWAT team there for several years and had graduated from the FBI Academy in Quantico. He was tall, slim and balding. In a short-sleeved shirt, the muscles he developed in faithful sessions at the gym showed the slimness was deceptive. His way of supervising was quiet and understated. Beyond the "cop" facade of expressionless face and calm confidence, Howell had a dry wit and a charming smile. His intelligence and experience stood him in good stead in his new job with its vast responsibilities. The men who served under him liked and respected him. He worked long hours, staying at the office after the other supervisors went home. He had been a captain in the police department when Benny Parkey was elected county sheriff and invited him to lead the new team taking over the sheriff's office. Like most Texas sheriffs, Parkey was busy being an elected official. Traditionally, chief deputies do the heavy lifting when it comes to day-to-day operations. Parkey trusted Howell to make most of the decisions, but he always knew what was going on, and he always had the last word.

Sergeant Steve Macsas, who also had been at the crime scene, became assistant chief deputy. He too was muscular from hours at the gym and morning runs around his neighborhood. Both men looked good in their clothes, which never seemed to wrinkle. They were determined when they took over the sheriff's office to clean up what they believed was corruption fostered by the former sheriff. And they had learned some hard lessons at the Lozano house that they used to strengthen their new department. They made some mistakes because they trusted Bobby that night, they admitted, but vowed it would never happen again.

People watched to see what Sheriff Parkey and company would do with the department. They soon found out. Parkey had a list of employees who'd worked at the sheriff's office because the former sheriff wanted them there for support. They were people the previous sheriff had felt he could trust. They were people who'd helped him build a home on land in East Texas.

After his election, Parkey personally went to about two dozen employees. In each case he explained that he could document something they had done under the former sheriff that would merit losing their jobs, and he told them he would not need them when he took office. He became known as the grim reaper in those weeks between the election and the date of his swearing in as the new sheriff. When Parkey walked into a room, it quickly emptied. But he found the people he wanted to fire and gave them the news himself. He replaced them with people he believed to be competent officers. He demanded total integrity from his employees and fired anyone who did not comply. In Howell and Macsas, he felt he had a team he could depend on. And he did depend on them.

Many of those fired appealed to the US Equal Employment Opportunity Commission. They claimed they had been fired because of age discrimination. Parkey sent along his reply to that, complete with explanations for the reasons they were not being rehired for his administration. The EEOC upheld every firing.

It was amazing how fast Parkey, Howell and Macsas had been able to turn around a sheriff's office with such a poor image when they took over. By the time of the trial, the department's image was spotless.

Chief Deputy Howell walked into the courtroom after lunch on Thursday, July 23, 2009, looking calm and confident in his dark pin-striped suit. He had been frustrated when the original indictment against Bobby Lozano was dropped, but he'd believed Bruce Isaacks, then DA, when he'd said the case had been declared a suicide. He had not been sure that handing over the files to a reporter even six years later was a good idea, but once on board, he'd been helpful in explaining the nuances of the case and the behind-the-scenes details.

Howell had gained much more experience speaking before groups since his appointment as chief deputy; he knew the facts of the case and was not going to be deterred by Hagen's attempts to discredit the investigation. He was polite but firm with Hagen. But first, Cary Piel started by having Howell debunk Bobby's stories to his family that the SWAT team took him away from home for hours each week and most holidays and that he was a member of some covert agency task force. Bobby's mother-in-law and brother-in-law could not be dissuaded from this notion, but it was all just an elaborate cover for Bobby's affairs.

"To my knowledge, he was never assigned to any task force associated with the DEA," Howell said. "And he may have been called out on the SWAT team once every three months. Never on a holiday."

Bobby appeared nervous rather than grief stricken that night while the police were there, Howell said. He compared what he saw in Bobby's demeanor that night to two other prior instances in years past at the police department, where Howell had been Bobby's supervisor.

"He was very physically upset and almost in tears when he came to me to say he had to leave because his baby needed to go to the doctor," Howell said. "And when he came to my office and told me his father had been put in the hospital, he was actually crying."

Cary Piel moved on to the crime scene. Did you notice anything about Viki Lozano's leg? he asked.

"It was evident to me that her leg had been off the bed for a while," Howell replied.

"Tell us about a shored gunshot wound. What does that mean?" Piel asked.

"With a shored gunshot wound, the bullet passes through soft tissue and stops against something firm."

So if the wound was shored, it meant that Viki wasn't in the sitting position Bobby said he found her in when she died. When she was shot, she would have been lying on her left side?

Right, Howell agreed. The best word he could think of for the scene was "staged," he said. It was not natural, and it could not have been that way when the bullet was fired.

In the first place, no one cleans a gun on the bed. It's a dirty job, and you certainly would not eat popcorn while doing it. Aside from the mess, the transfer of the gun oil to the popcorn would make it taste bad, and the transfer of the salt and butter from the popcorn to the gun would be really bad for the Glock. Also, a single sheet of newspaper would not protect the expensive bedding from the oil and gunshot residue. It would soak through the newspaper quickly. And as for the oil on the gun, it appeared as though someone had just taken a can and sprayed far more oil than was necessary all over the gun.

Furthermore, there was transfer blood from the sheets to the coverlet, which had been turned back after some blood had already soaked into the sheet, Howell said. The newspaper had been placed on top of that, and the gun-cleaning kit on top of the newspaper. They found the shell casing underneath all that in a fold of the spread. That meant that everything on top of it had been placed there after the gun was fired.

"Was there any sense among the detectives of 'We're going to get Bobby Lozano?'" Piel asked.

"Nothing could be farther from the truth. We made every effort to make it as easy as possible on Bobby. We allowed the family to stay on the other side of the house. Today, if I had the chance to do it differently, I would have asked the family to leave and I would have roped off the whole house as a crime scene. But it was not until I read the statement from Bobby that I began to believe he was not telling us the truth and that things didn't add up," Howell said.

According to Howell's testimony, Cindy Waters showed up in his office the following Monday morning. She was upset, he said, and she poured out her story of the affair with Bobby, his promises to leave his wife and their plans to marry. She had concluded that Viki committed suicide, and she was guilt ridden about her part in that. Subsequently, she gave two more statements, each containing more details.

Nearly three weeks into the investigation, Howell had not heard from Anna Farish, he said. He thought he had an obligation to keep her abreast of the course the investigation was taking, and he called her son, David, and asked him to bring her into the office.

"I thought she'd have a lot of questions," he testified. "But she didn't. She told me she'd heard a lot of ugly rumors making it seem like more than an accident. She said rumors were that Bobby was involved. She blamed the police department for that and said she wanted it stopped."

Hagen then took over the questioning. He began with

everything he could think of that Howell hadn't ordered done at the crime scene. Did he order anyone to test Bobby's hands for gunshot residue? Did he order someone to photograph Bobby's hands?

"Did you order his car searched? Did you check the Dumpsters on the route from the tanning salon? Did you check trash receptacles near the house?" Hagen continued his machine-gun, rapid-fire questioning style.

Howell held a calm facade, but inside he was likely seething. There were good explanations for his answering every question in the negative, but Hagen was asking yes-or-no questions, and it would sound defensive if Howell attempted to blurt out explanations. Hagen's technique didn't allow Howell time to explain.

The defense attorney also quizzed Howell about the diagram that Jeff Wawro had made using his personal software program. The diagram showed the shell casing located north of the cleaning kit, Howell acknowledged. But that was because the program did not have the 3-D capacity to show it underneath the kit where it had been found. Nevertheless, Hagen referred to this flawed diagram over and over to bolster his theory that the police had lied about where they'd found the shell casing, and there was no proof it had been found in the location they claimed it had turned up.

Hagen began to ask about the Chicago medical examiner's report, and Piel instantly objected. Judge McFarling sent the jury out, and the lawyers argued, not for the first time and not for the last time, over any mention of that report to the jury. Piel argued that if Hagen wanted to introduce Dr. Donaghue's opinion, he could call him to the witness stand. Hagen argued that he had a certified copy of Bruce Isaacks's sworn affidavit as to Donaghue's opinion and that it should be entered into evidence so he could talk about it. The judge ruled that for now, the affidavit would not come into evidence and no one would mention the report in front of the jury.

While they were waiting for the jury to return to the jury box, Cary Piel stood close to Howell, and they talked in low voices. With the jury seated, Hagen's first question to Howell was, "What was the prosecutor talking to you about when he was all up in your ear?"

Piel jumped to his feet. McFarling sent the jury out.

"This is ridiculous," Piel said.

McFarling sustained his objection to the way the question was asked but allowed Hagen to ask about the conversation. It was about the origin of the diagram, Howell said.

Hagen bore down on Howell about the two reports, one from an officer and one from a paramedic, that mentioned that Viki had both legs hanging off the bed. Hagen implied that the paramedics must've moved the body when they arrived, and then someone moved it back. That would account for two people seeing two legs hanging off the bed and others seeing only one.

Howell was adamant that the body was not moved.

"Do officers make mistakes when they write reports?" Piel asked him on redirect.

"Absolutely," Howell replied. "It frequently happens."

Bobby's own statement said one foot was hanging off the bed, he said.

Through the testimony Bobby sat quietly. He took notes. He occasionally pushed his notebook over to show to Hagen. He never looked around at his family. During breaks he talked to his sister. He seemed detached from Renee, whose questioning eyes would have been hard to meet. They spent time together during long breaks like lunch, and they left together every day. Bobby's family, especially Frank and his wife, were protective of Renee. She had no one in the courtroom except the Lozano family. She was tense and stiff most of the time while Bobby sat directly in front of her, separated by the bar, and seemed to ignore her.

James Willingham had been a computer analyst with the district attorney's office at the time of the investigation. He took the witness stand after Howell and explained that he had examined Bobby's home computer and also his computer at the police department as part of the investigation. Piel began questioning by talking about Bobby's statement. Bobby said he had been playing a game on the computer for about an hour that night before deciding to clean his gun and then changing his mind. He couldn't remember the exact name of the game, according to his statement.

Willingham testified that a game called Super Mahjongg had been running on the computer from July 2 until police unplugged it to take to the department. There was no evidence, however, that the game was played at all on the day Viki died. The computer was not used for any purpose, he said, after the morning before Viki's death. The game was running but not being played. When you play a game, it leaves numerous "artifacts" on the hard drive, he said. There were no artifacts to back up Bobby's statement that he played on the computer before going to the tanning salon.

Hagen's main target took the stand early Friday morning, July 24, and testified for most of the day. Jeff Wawro, now a captain with the sheriff's office, had been the detective who "caught" the case by virtue of being on call that night. It was actually Bobby's night to be on call, but he had asked Wawro to work for him.

As lead investigator on the case, Wawro knew he would come under Hagen's gun. He also knew that Viki's mother, Anna Farish, had told people he was "after Bobby" because Wawro's strict religion damned philanderers. He decided he was not going to flinch under cross-examination, and it made for an interesting day in the courtroom.

Cary Piel led him through the investigation. He asked him about cleaning the gun on top of the bed.

"The quality of that home made it improbable at best," Wawro said.

A Glock, made mostly of a special plastic that won't even burn, self-lubricates and needs only a couple of drops of oil on the metal workings. Excess oil collects dust and makes a mess that gums up the workings of the gun, he said. A police officer knows better. Any gun owner would know better. There was oil dripping out the barrel and out the slide and dripping down the side of the gun.

Through this Bobby remained stone-faced and still. He had not seemed to react at all to the damning stories of his girlfriends or the critical statements of his former coworkers. Wawro's testimony seemed inconsequential to him. His police training, perhaps, helped him keep a calm facade.

Piel brought Wawro off the witness stand and over to the large photo of the crime scene with Viki still on the bed. He began asking him questions about the positions of various things while Wawro pointed them out. Hagen and Bobby moved to the left side of the jury box so they could see the photo, which had been placed directly in front of the jury. The location put Wawro between Hagen and the photo. Hagen asked Wawro to move, and then he asked the judge to make him move so he could see better.

"Judge, the counselor can move," Cary Piel said in exasperation. "I need my witness to be able to show this to the jury."

McFarling gestured, and Hagen moved to the other side of the jury box.

Then, despite the tragic circumstances he was emulating, Piel had everyone smiling as he maneuvered his middle-aged, slightly overweight body down onto the floor and into the position Viki would have had to be lying in to have the shored gunshot exit wound on her left side. He grasped the Glock in his right hand and looked over his shoulder at Wawro.

"Have you ever cleaned a gun lying on your side like this?" he asked.

"No," Wawro said, and Piel struggled to his feet, his point well made.

They went over the bloody partial print on the bottom of the cleaning solution can. Wawro agreed that someone touched Viki's blood and then moved the can. Viki didn't do that, he said. Someone else moved the can after she died.

They addressed the popcorn in her mouth and down the front of her pajamas. There was no bowl or bag of popcorn in sight anywhere in the bedroom. If Viki had walked across the house to the kitchen to put the popcorn away, surely the popcorn kernels would have fallen out of the loose pajama shirt, he said. Instead, the kernels were stuck in the blood around her wound.

Piel asked Wawro about the shell casing. The investigators did not touch the bed until after the medical examiner investigator arrived. But they did search for the shell casing under and behind the bed. They looked in the folds of the silken drapes around the canopy frame of the bed. Then finally, after the body was gone, they lifted things off the bed layer by layer until they came to the folds of the blanket. Slowly, they smoothed out the folds, and there was the shell casing. The newspaper and the cleaning kit had been on top of it all along.

"It would be highly unlikely for that casing to pass through the box and get where we found it," Wawro said.

Wawro also talked about CPR. He said he timed the moments on the 911 tape between when Bobby said he was going to put the baby down and start CPR and when he came back to the telephone.

"'I'm going to do CPR right now. I'm going to set my baby down.' Twenty-five seconds later he was back asking where the ambulance was," Wawro said. "The phone is in the alcove and he could see the bed. He said in his statement that the baby was crying. But you don't hear a crying baby on the 911 tape."

After the midmorning break, Piel played the 911 tape for the jurors with Wawro still on the stand. Wawro testified that Bobby's statement said, "I begged her not to die, not to leave us alone." But there was nothing on the 911 tape to show that he said that.

Hagen took over for cross-examination. He brought out a flip chart of white paper and began writing on it as Wawro answered questions. Cary Piel objected. That was not proper, he said. Hagen said he wanted the flip chart to refer to when he was giving his summation to the jury. It wasn't proper for Hagen to write something in his own way and then tell the jury that was testimony, Piel said. The judge agreed, and Hagen reluctantly put the flip chart away. His frustration at having his prop removed was evident.

Hagen bore in on Wawro about the computer-rendered diagram, which at this point everyone privately said they wished Wawro had never made. He told Wawro he understood that the software program had limitations but asked him if there hadn't been some better way, if indeed the casing was under the kit, of showing that. He could have drawn a line, perhaps?

"Is it your testimony today that the casing was under the box?"

"Yes," Wawro said.

"Show the jury where you documented that the casing was under the kit," Hagen said. "Show us anywhere in the world that you stated the casing was found under the kit."

Hagen insisted that the evidence list should show evidence in the order it was taken from the bed. Wawro explained that the detectives first moved everything to the foot of the bed and then placed it into evidence, so the order did not reflect a true rendering of the way it was removed from the places they found it.

"Let's talk about meticulous evidence collecting," Hagen said. "Assuming that the casing was found on top of the kit . . ."

"I'd rather not do that," Wawro interjected. "It was not found on top."

The counselor and the witness clashed on several other topics after that, Wawro not giving an inch on his testimony despite Hagen's onslaught of questions. The defense attorney showed Wawro two enlarged photos of the bed with some of the evidence still on it.

"Do you see how the tiger eye [on the blanket design] has moved between the photos?" he asked.

"That's what you're not understanding, counselor," Wawro cut in, but Hagen objected and Wawro was not allowed to finish. "I can explain that . . ." Wawro tried again, and again Hagen cut him off.

Finally, the judge called a lunch break, and Wawro stepped off the stand with a look of relief. But there was still the afternoon.

Hagen started right in after the lunch break with the bruises on Viki's hands and legs. There were several, some old, some so new they only appeared after the body was taken to the morgue. But Hagen was interested in only two. There was a small, fresh bruise at the base of the right thumb. Hagen wanted the jury to believe Viki suffered this bruise when she fired the weapon. He grilled Wawro on the bruise. Wawro would not cooperate with the theory, even though Hagen questioned him over and over. He didn't remember the medical examiner putting a time frame on that bruise, he said. He didn't know when it occurred. The bite of a pistol slide held improperly while firing doesn't hit the base of the thumb. It cuts the web of the hand. He did not believe that firing a gun caused the bruise. He also disagreed with Hagen that the L-shaped bruise on Viki's forehead was caused when the pistol recoiled and the side of the Glock hit her head. A recoil would not go in that direction. Finally, Hagen gave up on Wawro, and Cary Piel started trying to clear up what he felt Hagen had muddied over.

As to the diagram: In all the diagrams, the shell casing actually was in the proper place, wasn't it? he asked Wawro. Yes. It was the cleaning kit box that was not in its proper place on the diagrams, Wawro explained. The diagrams were not meant to be to scale. It was just a convenient way of illustrating the crime scene for the investigators' own use, he said.

Wawro also showed the jury what he said was wrong with the two photographs that Hagen insisted showed things had been moved. It wasn't the items that had moved, Wawro told the jury. It was the angle of the photograph taken that distorted distances. Additionally, the two photographs had been taken at different times during evidence collection to document the process. He told the jurors to stick their thumbs up and look at them first with both eyes, then with one eye and then the other closed. It wasn't the photo that moved, he explained. It was the perspective.

The touted "defense exhibit number ten" had been debunked.

Cary Piel took a marking pen and drew a bruise on the back of his thumb. Then he held the gun in different ways, some of them ludicrous. None of them would have caused the bruise, he demonstrated. When the slide "bites" when it flies back during firing, it normally cuts the web of the hand, between the thumb and forefinger. The bruise on the back of the thumb was in the wrong place.

Piel placed the butt of the gun against the bruise on a life-sized blowup of Viki's forehead. If the defendant hit the victim in the head with the butt of the gun before he shot her, would that match the bruise? he asked Wawro. Yes, it would, the detective replied.

Wawro stepped from the witness stand, looking tired but relieved. He had gambled by tussling with the defense attorney. He'd told the lawyer he was wrong. It was not a standard way for a police officer to testify. If Hagen had strenuously objected to those tactics, the judge likely would have ordered Wawro to simply answer the questions. Hagen didn't, though, and Wawro won the round.

CHAPTER 18

DOGS ON THE BED AND LEGS OFF THE BED

Denton police officer Dale Binkert, the next witness that day, was a big guy: six feet four inches tall, broad but not fat. He towered over prosecutor Cary Piel in the courtroom so much that he seemed larger than life. He was a veteran police officer, and he knew what to do. His report was brief, and so was his time on the witness stand. He had been the first officer on the scene, but the fire department was already there when he arrived. He'd walked briefly into the room and stood at the foot of the bed, he said. Then he walked outside and asked the second arriving officer, Rachel Key, to write down the names of anyone entering or exiting the bedroom. He radioed to ask that the detective on call be notified that he needed to come to the house on La Mancha as quickly as possible.

In answer to Cary Piel's questions, "Bink," as his fellow patrol officers called him, said he saw no dogs in the room.

He said that once out of the room he never entered it again.

Hagen tried to question Binkert about the number of Viki's legs he saw hanging off the bed. He never rounded the bed to see from that angle, he said. He didn't know whether one or both of her legs were hanging off the bed.

———————

Officer Rachel Key, now Detective Rachel Key Fleming, was to prove troubling for the prosecution as a witness. In the intervening years since Viki Lozano died, Rachel Key had married prosecutor Jeff Fleming. It was embarrassing for her to have to admit to Piel that her report was inaccurate, but it would get worse during cross-examination. Cary Piel knew this and began by addressing one of the problems himself. Key's report stated that she'd seen both of Viki's legs hanging off the bed and that both demonstrated lividity.

"It was a long night," she said on the stand. She had written the report hours after seeing the body. "I thought I'd seen two legs. But after I talked to the other officers I realized that I had made a mistake."

Only one of the victim's legs dangled off the bed, she testified that she now recalled.

Piel asked her if she ever talked to Bobby that night. She tried to, Key said. She was told by a supervisor to let Bobby know that his pastor was on the way.

"When I went to Bobby, he stood up and looked at me and started walking rapidly away. I thought, 'He's running away from me.'"

Piel asked her about seeing the family dogs.

"I saw the dogs, which was why I entered the bedroom," she said. "They were little dogs. I call them 'yip-yip' dogs. They were on the bed but not near the body. They jumped down. Sergeant Creamer rounded them up and locked them in the bathroom."

"Did you ever see the dogs move anything on the bed?"

"No," she replied.

When it was his turn to question her, defense attorney Rick Hagen didn't play nice for very long. "Seven years ago you made an observation and wrote that both Virginia's feet were hanging off the bed and both had lividity. Now you think you didn't see that?"

Key agreed. Now she didn't think she saw that.

"Seven years ago you said that the dogs were on the bed licking the body."

"I don't believe I ever said that," she said.

"You told a district attorney's employee that you saw the dogs licking the body. The district attorney's employee made a note of the reference. Are you saying you didn't see that or that you didn't tell anyone that?"

"If someone made a note that I told them that, then I must have. But I don't recall seeing the dogs licking the blood on the body," she said.

Key left the stand, but on Monday, Hagen introduced a sworn affidavit signed by her that stated that she *had* told then assistant district attorney Tony Paul that she saw the dogs licking blood off the body. Hagen had scored a point for the defense.

Detective Jason Grellhesl was good-looking and personable, and since the time of Viki's death, he had been assigned to a federal drug task force under the auspices of the FBI that drew officers from area police departments. He was now based in Plano and was seldom around the police department. But he had been a member of the detective crime scene team, and he had helped gather evidence that night.

He was a veteran witness, and he didn't let Hagen trip him up.

He stated that he and Detective Craig Fitzgearld had walked through the whole house looking for anything unusual. They did not perform a full search of the whole house, but he said they did look briefly in every closet and every drawer. They found nothing noteworthy in the rest of the large house, he told Cary Piel.

In the bedroom, Grellhesl's first reaction was surprise at seeing the cleaning kit laid out on the bed.

"I questioned why someone would be cleaning a gun on a bed," he said. "It's something I've never done."

The gun was covered with "an exorbitant amount of oil," he said. He recovered the shell casing from the folds of the blanket and placed it in an empty film canister. He punched a hole in the top of the canister to "let it breathe."

Hagen began cross-examination by questioning him about the way Detective Russell Lewis's evidence should have been configured. Lewis was the detective assigned to work the crime scene. He shot photographs and entered evidence into a log. He was in charge of taking the evidence back to the police department and placing it in the secure evidence room. Wasn't it true that Lewis, the crime scene detective, would have listed evidence in the order that it was recovered?

"I couldn't testify to Detective Lewis's report," Grellhesl responded, deftly avoiding the intent of the question.

Lewis had left the department by then and had moved to another state. He was not subpoenaed for the trial.

Then Grellhesl handled the loaded question Hagen put another way about the evidence being logged in the order that it was collected.

"It can't have been in order," Grellhesl said. "Because the shell casing comes before the kit and newspaper on the list, and that's not the way we collected it."

Hagen gave up on the court-savvy detective but reserved the right to question him again. He never did.

Detective Craig "Fitz" Fitzgearld was a sandy-haired, mild-looking man of about forty who appeared like he could have been an accountant but was in fact acknowledged as one of the most "kick-ass" officers on the force. If trouble was there, so was Fitz. He had an eye for things that just didn't look right and a way of talking to people that elicited guilty information. He made arrests on his way to work in the mornings. He was restless when he was at his desk, saying to anyone who seemed to have nothing to do, "Come on. Let's go arrest someone." Arresting people with outstanding warrants was his main job. He was a member of what was fondly called the RAT (recidivism action team). He and another officer roamed the streets looking for trouble, and they served warrants, successfully searching out the hiding places of wanted men and women. Fitzgearld had once been forced to kill a dog that was attacking him while he struggled with the dog's owner. He tased the man and shot the dog. And he'd once killed a man in the line of duty, shooting him as they struggled on the ground. The other man was trying to stab him with a syringe. Fitzgearld's normally soft heart hardened when he put on his badge, but the dead man haunted him.

On the witness stand, Fitzgearld echoed Grellhesl's memories of the night. They had acted as a team in going over the rest of the house looking for anything out of place. He had helped straighten the tiger blanket to retrieve the shell casing from its folds.

When he was looking around the house, the defense attorney asked, would a popcorn bag have been something he would have considered out of place? Fitzgearld said he didn't see a popcorn bag but that he wouldn't have considered it out of place then, since he didn't know about the popcorn kernels in the bed and on the victim at that time.

After Detective Craig Fitzgearld, Todd Eddington took the stand. He had been the manager of the Planet Tan salon the night Viki died and Bobby came in to tan. Cary Piel used him to verify a document the state had subpoenaed from the salon. It showed the record of Bobby's visits to the business. For months he had been visiting once a week. But the night his wife died was Bobby's second visit in two days. He came in at 8:26 P.M. on July 6 and stayed in the tanning bed for twenty minutes, chatting afterward with Eddington for a moment about how he'd celebrated the Fourth of July. It was the first time Bobby had ever spoken to him, the manager said.

The last witness of the day was Teresa Starrett. Starrett was the principal of one school where Viki had taught, and she had worked as a teacher with her at another school earlier. Susan and Cary Piel intended to send the jurors home for the weekend thinking about their victim.

She was an amazing teacher, Starrett said of Viki. "She was highly individualized, extremely in tune with the students' needs."

Starrett testified that Viki had been thrilled to be pregnant with her son, Monty, and happy afterward.

"She was so filled with joy. She was so in love with him. He really changed her. She was absolutely enraptured by that child."

Susan Piel asked Starrett about Viki's decision to take a year off from school to be with her baby boy. Starrett remembered the last day of school that year when Viki was packing up her room to leave.

"She was so happy. I remember that she had this beautiful vase and she gave it to a colleague. That is my last memory of her," Starrett said. "Her happiness and her gift of that beautiful vase."

The trial was over for the day.

CHAPTER 19

A CRAMMED COURTROOM

I was tired, having worked thirteen- to fourteen-hour days all week. Each morning I handed a flash drive to a photographer hired by *48 Hours* news program, which was considering doing a show about the trial. At noon, he downloaded the photographs he'd taken that morning to the drive, and I was responsible for getting the photos to my newspaper office. At first, I took the flash drive home and while gobbling a sandwich I uploaded them to my computer, picked out the best shots and e-mailed them to the editor. I'd then hand the photographer a fresh flash drive before the afternoon session began and repeat the selection process when I got home. The newspaper photographers decided that I might not be picking the best shots. They wanted to do that. So the next week someone met me outside the courtroom and picked up the flash drive. The staff photographers got to choose the photos we used, and I wasn't always happy when they left out photos I thought better represented the events in court that day. But at least I hoped it would give me a chance to eat lunch. As it turned out, though, I still rarely had time to eat because I had to reclaim my seat half an hour before the judge walked back into the courtroom. If I didn't, I would not get a seat. I didn't want to miss a minute of testimony, so I started just bringing a bottle of water and some small candy bars to carry me through.

As each day of the trial passed, seating in the small courtroom became more precious. People who read my daily stories wanted to watch the drama for themselves. But as usual, courthouse personnel who worked in other parts of the building left their desks and took up at least half the seating at any given time. Would-be spectators lined the benches outside in the hall hoping for someone to leave so they could grab the seat. I began arriving earlier and earlier to ensure a seat with a good view of both the witness stand and the jury. Sometimes I didn't get that, but I always managed to sit somewhere.

But seating was at a real premium. One day, I heard the courtroom door open behind me and two men I knew well walked in. Narcotics sergeant Brad Curtis and narcotics officer Danny Fletcher scanned the room for a bit of space to sit down. Narcotics officers are different. They have to be to deal with the criminals they handle every day. They know just how far they can go, and they march right up to that line. I had worked with Curtis when he was a criminal investigation sergeant, and Fletcher was in his office every day. They treated me like one of the guys, and I took that as a compliment. Nothing embarrassed me, and it was a good thing.

Fletcher spotted a tiny gap between me and the woman next to me. He inserted himself into the gap. He wasn't a tall man. In his narcotics casual disguise he looked about sixteen years old. He managed to squeeze in. Then Curtis decided to sit on the end of my bench, even though there now was not one inch of room. He gave me a shove with his hip, mashing me against Fletcher. Trying to stifle my giggles, I took notes with my arms out in front of me. There simply wasn't room for them on the bench. I hoped the judge wouldn't blame me for the interruption. He knew those guys and cut them—and me—some slack.

The next witness did not hold the narcotics guys' attention, and soon they were back out the door, leaving me with room to take a deep breath.

———————

One of the other issues with sitting in court was the inability to use cell phones. Once, when Detective Craig Fitzgearld had just taken the stand, the ring of a cell phone startled the courtroom full of people. Cell phones were not allowed to ring. If yours rang, you were in trouble. You were in contempt of court. There was a hefty fine. I couldn't tell whose phone rang, but it was near me. The bailiff stood and beckoned to a man sitting in my row. He slowly rose and walked to the bar where the bailiff stood. There was a whispered conversation. The man handed over his phone. Then he reached in his pocket and pulled out his wallet. He handed over his driver's license. After another whispered conversation he returned to his seat. Proceedings began again. After court closed for the day, the man stood before the judge and was charged with contempt of court. The offending man never returned to the courtroom after that.

It only reinforced my worry about committing the same error. I usually checked my phone two or three times after I returned from a break. The fine wouldn't be good, I thought. But the humiliation of having that happen before a courtroom full of people would be worse.

A couple of days earlier I had heard the telltale ring from the purse of an elderly woman sitting next to me. That time, neither the judge nor the bailiff was in the courtroom. She reached in her handbag and began searching for it as it steadily rang.

"You have to turn it off. You'll get in trouble," I said to her.

"I don't know how to turn it off!" she wailed. She held it like it was a cobra as it continued to trill.

"Give it to me," I told her. I dashed out of the courtroom just as the judge entered, and I turned off the incriminating piece of electronics in the hallway. It had been close. I returned it to the grateful woman, hoping she wouldn't bring it back the next day.

After Teresa Starrett's testimony that Friday, July 24, I was exhausted, but I headed to the office to write my story so that I could finally use the weekend to get some rest.

The *Record-Chronicle* website, where my stories led the slate every day, was busy with readers commenting on the stories and expressing their opinions. We had never had so many comments on the stories. We had never had such arguing among the writers. Our editors had to keep a constant watch on the comments section under my stories. Some of the writers got nasty. Some of the comments were libelous. Those had to be removed as soon as possible.

That weekend, one writer was furious because there was no new story on the trial. He implied that I had gotten lazy and deprived him of his daily read. Other readers tried to explain that there was no trial taking place on the weekend, but he didn't seem to think that was a good enough excuse for my dereliction.

On Monday, I was back at the courthouse gathering fodder for his Lozano trial fix.

CHAPTER 20

THE SECOND WEEK

It was Monday morning, July 27, 2009, the second week of the trial. All the players already looked tired, as though they had worked all weekend on the case. Bobby Lozano was turned out, as usual, in a well-cut suit. He looked exhausted, and something in his eyes signaled fear, though he kept his face composed. Renee Lozano was wearing pants with a top made of luxe material. She was plainly frightened. She was learning details she'd never heard before, and they conflicted deeply with the story of Bobby's first wife's death that he had recounted to her. Photographs taken during the trial from the front of the courtroom showed a woman watching her world turn dark. She still sat in the front row, and more and more of Bobby's relatives surrounded her, holding her hand or encircling her shoulders for support. The family obviously was facing the very real possibility of conviction.

The courtroom was even more crowded than it had been the previous week, with people squeezing into the benches, shoulder jammed against shoulder.

It was Texas Ranger Tracy Murphree's turn in the witness box.

Texas Rangers traditionally wear their badges on their shirts, and Murphree's was there on his starched and pressed Western-cut shirt. They often wear tooled leather belts and holsters. Tracy's had been made by inmates of the Texas prison system. Rangers always wear white straw or silver belly hats, which are their winter head covering of gray felt made by premier Western hatmaker, the Stetson company. His was resting in his seat just behind the prosecutors. Hatless, Murphree was balding and seldom removed the Stetson. So courtroom spectators saw him as few strangers did. But court protocol mandated the hat be removed, so a bit of his Ranger persona was lost. He wasn't a tall man, but he stood straight with perfect law enforcement posture. He was amiable with his friends and formidable to criminals.

Murphree testified that in his years as a Texas Highway patrolman and then a Ranger he had been to approximately 150 death scenes. Rangers begin as Highway Patrol officers and work their way through the ranks to the top position as one of the fabled Texas Rangers.

He said that Bobby had been allowed to come to his office at the Texas Department of Public Safety local headquarters to make his statement about his wife's death two days afterward as a favor because he was a fellow law enforcement officer whose wife had died. It was better, the officers thought, than having to come to his place of work during this time. Texas Ranger Tony Bennie was also there, as well as Denton detective Mike Bateman, who had been a friend of Bobby's and wanted to give him support.

"[Bobby] was allowed to type his own statement, and he did it on my computer," Murphree testified.

When he read Bobby's statement, though, Murphree was not comfortable with his explanation of cleaning the gun on the bed. It didn't make sense, the Ranger said. And Bobby had said that his wife was tired and not feeling well, so why would she decide to take on that chore?

The oil on the Glock was most disconcerting.

"If you are experienced with a gun, you wouldn't put that much oil on it, and you certainly would not hold it facing your body," he told Cary Piel. "And if you are not experienced with a gun, then you don't handle it."

Bobby's statement said he left his gun unloaded and locked open. So Viki would have had to load it before cleaning it. Absolutely not, Murphree said.

Besides, Viki had no oil on her hands.

"I held her hands in my hands to look for oil, and there was none," he testified.

The Ranger said he asked Bobby when he was at Murphree's office to show him the position he found his wife in when he walked in the bedroom door. Bobby had sat in his chair and leaned over his left knee. If he was telling the truth, Murphree said, he would have expected to see lividity in Viki's face, since that would've been a low point where blood would pool. There was none.

The popcorn also troubled him. Who eats popcorn while cleaning a smelly, dirty gun? "You don't want to get salt in your gun, and you don't want to get oil on your popcorn. It's in her mouth, it's in her clothing, it's in her bed. She was eating popcorn. But where was the bowl?"

Then there was the transfer blood on the covers that had been folded back, he said. There was blood *under* the newspaper, but no blood *on* the newspaper. There was a bloody fingerprint smudge on the bottom of the oilcan. Someone other than Viki had touched it after she was shot.

"I believe the crime scene was staged," he said.

The gunshot residue on her pajama sleeves didn't mean that Viki had fired the gun. It could simply mean that her sleeves were in proximity to the gun when it was fired.

"If I have my hands up like this," Cary Piel said, putting his hands up in a defensive position, "would you expect to find gunshot residue on my sleeve?"

Yes, the Ranger answered. He believed Viki's arms had been thrown up in defense when the gun went off. There had been a struggle, he believed. He couldn't say just when she was hit by the butt of the gun or if the blow actually knocked her unconscious. Probably not. There was a lot going on during that struggle, as evidenced by bruises on her arms and even her legs.

Tracy Murphree had brought to court a video demonstration of the way Viki's body was removed from the room. Cary Piel moved to show it to the jury. Hagen objected. The Ranger hadn't made the video. The person who did had had no personal knowledge of the way the body would have been removed. That person was not present then. Cary Piel responded that the video matched the physical evidence exactly. Judge McFarling sustained the objection, and Hagen won that round. The jury did not see the video.

Cary Piel instead played a short tape from a surveillance camera at the Target store in Lewisville, Texas, that showed Bobby and Viki checking out. It did not show them laughing at the toys in the basket, as Bobby had claimed in his statement.

Piel then turned to the bruises on Viki's hand and forehead, as he had with Jeff Wawro. When you hold a pistol too loosely and the slide hits your hand, does it hit the base of the thumb? he asked the Ranger. Murphree demonstrated that there was no way to hold a Glock that would put the slide in contact with the base of the thumb. What about the mark on Viki's forehead? If she was holding the gun in the position she would've had to in order to make the wound on her chest, would the gun have recoiled into her forehead? No, Murphree said. The recoil would be in the opposite direction. The bruise was more consistent with someone hitting her with the butt of the gun. Piel and the Ranger stood before the jury to demonstrate.

"Murder me again," Piel said to Murphree, indicating he wanted the Ranger to pretend to shoot him. The implication was not wasted on the spectators.

Murphree stated that 99 percent of all suicides by firearm are contact wounds. People tended to press the gun against their flesh to steady it for firing. In this case, the gun was fired three to six inches away from her body. It was in a really awkward position for her to have fired it, he said.

"If she were going to kill herself, would it be consistent for her to clean it first?" Piel asked.

No, Murphree answered. It wouldn't. "If his statement is true, there would have had to be a series of impossible or improbable things that happened," he said.

After the midmorning break, Rick Hagen took over questioning the Ranger. He first asked for the report from the night of Viki Lozano's death. But Murphree had not made a report. Ranger Tony Bennie had been the technical case manager, and while he *had* made a report, it was unavailable to Hagen because Bennie never testified. Exactly why Bennie was never called to the stand was unclear. Perhaps there was something in that report that the prosecution would rather not have brought out; perhaps it was as simple as the fact that Bennie had been promoted and no longer worked in the area. Hagen could have subpoenaed Bennie himself, but he didn't.

Wasn't it true that methods of determining a time of death, such as rigor mortis or lividity, were not 100 percent reliable? Hagen asked the Ranger. Murphree amiably conceded that was true. And wasn't it true that about 75 percent of suicides don't leave notes? That also was true, Murphree said. And wasn't it true that a suicide could be masked as a gun cleaning?

"I haven't seen it in my experience," he replied.

The defense attorney questioned Murphree about several aspects of the collection of evidence. Could it have been done a little better?

Sure, the Ranger said.

Hagen went through a series of questions designed to make the investigation look shoddy. Did you have the 911 tape enhanced? No. Were you able to determine when Viki put the popcorn in her mouth? No. Did anyone search Bobby's car? Not to the Ranger's knowledge. No one checked the Dumpsters on the way to the tanning salon? No. No one took photographs or tested Bobby's hands? No. Denton Police Department gunshot residue testing kits were expired; but couldn't you have gotten one from some other agency in the county? They did not.

Hagen picked apart the police reports, spending a lot of time showing that no one had documented finding the shell casing under the cleaning kit. And he asked about reports or supplements in any year since 2002. Did anyone ever specifically document the shell casing being found under the kit? The answer was no.

Cary Piel took over in redirect questioning. The detectives photographed the shell casing being found under the kit, did they not, he asked Murphree. Yes, they did. And if the dogs had been on the bed, would their weight have caused the casing to roll under the kit? No. It would have rolled into the depression the dogs made.

Piel asked about the paramedic who had written in his report that both Viki's legs were hanging off the bed. Did he write that he was the last one out of the room? No. And wasn't he also the paramedic who wrote in his report that Viki was wearing a long white nightgown? Yes, he was that same paramedic. His report was sloppy. Viki had been wearing pajamas.

———————

Dr. Gary Sisler was in his late seventies but still performing autopsies at the Tarrant County Medical Examiner's Office. He was funny and bright, and people who knew him well called him "Pops." He testified that he had performed in excess of four thousand autopsies in his career. The gunshot wound on Viki Lozano's body was right to left, downward, and front to back, he said. The exit wound was "abraded" or shored. The bullet traveled through her body and was stopped by the firm mattress so that it broke her skin, causing a sort of rim to the wound. It stopped there and remained inside her pajama top. She died of exsanguination—bleeding to death, much of the bleeding internal.

Sisler testified that he found no gun oil on Viki's hands.

He did find healing bruises all over her body. Some were on her legs and some on her hands. He also found some fresh bruises as well. He found partially digested popcorn in her stomach.

Hagen took over questioning. Based on forensic evidence, you could not tell whether the death was homicide, suicide or accidental? he asked.

The doctor said that was correct.

"You are still of the opinion that the manner of death is undetermined?"

That was also correct, Sisler agreed.

"There is no forensic evidence to show that Bobby had the gun in his hand?"

Sisler said the autopsy wasn't designed for that and he could not say.

Cary Piel asked Sisler if he had any knowledge about another opinion that the death might be suicide.

"I spoke to Dr. Donaghue on the telephone, and he agreed with me that you can't tell by the autopsy," the pathologist said.

Apparently, at some point after the first indictment had been dismissed, Sisler had called Chicago to discuss the case with Donaghue. He hadn't gotten too far himself with the enigmatic pathologist, who never did testify in the trial.

But the telephone call was important as far as the former district attorney's reasons for dropping the case years earlier. Had the Chicago medical examiner told Bruce Isaacks that he believed the death was a suicide, or hadn't he? And if not, why did Isaacks sign a sworn affidavit stating that he did? It seemed impossible that Isaacks could escape getting into some sort of trouble over this.

Piel did not bring Donaghue to testify. Hagen made a lot of noise about Donaghue, but he didn't put him on the witness stand either. Isaacks never would explain his reasons for asking for an opinion from the Chicago pathologist in the first place. The entire Donaghue issue was vague and confusing, and it remained so.

Sisler ended his testimony with one more piece of important evidence. Gunshot residue can be washed off or wiped off someone's hands and will not show up on sub-sequent tests. That information, even if it didn't excuse the police not testing Bobby's hands that night, at least rendered the point moot. Bobby had been immaculate when the paramedics arrived. He had most certainly washed off any evidence.

CHAPTER 21

SCIENTIFIC EVIDENCE

Constance Patton was the next witness. She too worked for the medical examiner's office as a DNA analyst. The DNA of the blood on the oilcan showed it was Viki's, she said. She looked for blood on the clothing Bobby had taken off at the detectives' request and found none. She had found a hair in the muzzle of the gun, but there was not enough DNA in it to test. She found no blood on the cleaning kit itself.

Patricia Eddings was a trace analyst at the medical examiner's office. She testified that Viki's body was very bloody but that Bobby's clothing had no blood on it at all.

The gun was so oily, Eddings said, that it had even left an oily ring on the paper they were storing it on the next day.

Dr. Monica Popov was an ob-gyn at a Denton women's clinic. She testified next, saying she took care of Viki Lozano during her pregnancy. Prosecutor Susan Piel asked her if Viki had ever had leukemia, as Bobby had told one of his mistresses. No, there was no indication that Viki ever had cancer, Popov said. Bobby came with Viki on some visits. His main interest, Popov recalled, seemed to be his wife's weight.

"He made a comment about her gaining too much weight. I reassured both of them that she was not gaining too much weight," Popov testified.

Viki told her doctor that she had once hemorrhaged after having a tooth extracted. So Popov referred her to a hematologist, but tests done at his office showed no blood disorder. Viki gave birth to her son on August 15, 2001. She experienced a minor tear, which often occurred during a vaginal delivery, the doctor testified. There was some small problem with the tear, but it was healed by the six-week checkup. The doctor never ordered bed rest for Viki. Popov said she had no indication Viki wasn't a normal mother caring for her baby in a normal way.

Viki Lozano had a normal pregnancy and a normal delivery, and her life was never in danger.

Susan Piel showed Popov part of Bobby's statement that read, "We knew that the possibility existed that she would not survive childbirth."

Not true, the doctor said.

Piel showed the doctor another paragraph that dealt

with the supposed reason no surgery was performed on the tear, which was a fear that "Viki was too weak to survive it."

"That is incorrect," Popov said.

Defense attorney Rick Hagen attacked the doctor's testimony in cross-examination.

"Do you know what Viki told Bobby about it?" he asked, and Popov allowed that she didn't.

So Bobby had woven an elaborate tangle of lies about Viki's health, her ability to care for her baby, her mental state. He told one girlfriend that Viki was dying of cancer, but not the next girlfriend. What was in his mind? How did he think these misconceptions on his girlfriends' parts would benefit him? Because everything he did and said was for his own benefit, there was no doubt of that. Were the lies that Viki was near death, either from leukemia or from impending childbirth, outward manifestations of Bobby's inner desires to have Viki's money without the inconvenience of living with her? Could anyone really explain why Bobby Lozano did or said anything? It seemed doubtful by now that even he could explain it.

Vicki Sargent had been a school administrator over Viki, who as a young mother also tutored Sargent's son in math. Sargent said she'd admired Viki's abilities and her dedication.

"She was a very committed teacher, very involved with her students. She was passionate and organized. She had it all together in that classroom," Sargent testified. The administrator worked with Viki first at Hodge Elementary and then at McNair, she said. Bobby would often visit school at lunchtime and bring Viki's lunch. Viki grew quiet when he was around.

In the school year of 1989–90, Viki came into Sargent's office one day. She'd sat down and pulled her knees up to her chest and wept, Sargent said.

"She said [she and Bobby] were separated. She was afraid of him. She believed he intended to do harm to some of her animals. She said to me, 'Bobby doesn't admit that he was wrong, ever.'" But soon the couple reconciled.

Sargent testified that a decade later, when Viki became pregnant and then after the baby was born, she was very happy. Viki had decided to stay home with her son the following school year, and she was joyous about that. But on July 8, 2002, Sargent learned the news that Viki was dead. Stunned, she visited the Lozano home to pay her respects. Bobby answered the door. He told her he didn't know what he would do without his wife, she said. He told Sargent that Viki had left a note on his steering wheel.

That note never surfaced, nor did anyone else ever hear of such a note.

Anna Farish seemed dazed, the administrator said. Sargent said that Anna told her how Viki had been planning a first birthday party for her son.

Anna also told her that Viki and Bobby had been eating popcorn that afternoon. Why would she tell her that? It was inexplicable that she would say it, and it could have only come from Bobby, since Anna wouldn't have even been there to see it. She did not arrive home until after Viki was dead.

Additionally, Sargent testified, Anna "told me the dogs had jumped on the bed and had somehow set off Bobby's service revolver." It was all very strange for her to say.

———————

After the lunch break on Monday, the jury was not at first allowed back into the courtroom. Hagen had some business to take care of. The motion to dismiss the case because it violated the speedy trial act was still moving along with the proceedings. Hagen would use all the testimony in the case to try to prove that his client's rights had been violated after the first indictment was dropped and another indictment was brought four years later. With the jury still away from the courtroom, former district attorney Bruce Isaacks took the stand. He had signed a sworn affidavit saying that Chicago medical examiner Edmund Donaghue sent a report stating he believed Viki's death was a suicide and that Dr. Sisler had agreed after learning of the report.

Isaacks wore his trademark black suit with a blue shirt and a red tie. His black hair seemed to have no more gray than when he was in office. His eyes, which had always had a slight bulge to them, were hard when he looked at prosecutor Cary Piel, who had once worked for him. When Paul Johnson won the top lawyer job in the county away from Isaacks, he'd rehired Cary Piel. Susan already had returned after her last baby.

Did Dr. Donaghue actually make a report? Cary Piel asked.

"He sent me a report that indicated he believed the death was a suicide," Isaacks said staunchly.

They had searched the records of the case carefully and there was no report, Piel said.

There was a multiple-page report, and it was in the file when he left office, Isaacks insisted.

"You are aware, are you not, that you're the only one who remembers a report?"

"No, I am not," Isaacks said.

Tony Paul, the prosecutor for the first case, didn't remember a report, Piel told Isaacks. Debra Bender, the first prosecutor assigned to the case, didn't remember a report. And Lee Ann Breading, his first assistant who was fully integrated into the case, said there was no report, Piel said. Breading had been involved from the beginning, attending all the meetings with police and the medical examiner. She even had talked about trying the case herself. She of all people should know if there was a report, and she had said there was none.

"She told me she didn't remember if there was a report or not," Isaacks countered. Privately, he later stated, "I can't help it if they lost that report."

Hagen had made arrangements for Isaacks to look at the case file, because he planned to call him as a witness, Piel said. Knowing that, why hadn't Isaacks come up to look at it? He had been contacted several times about it but never showed up.

"I tried," Isaacks claimed. "I sat in that office one afternoon but I couldn't get in to see anyone."

After that, Isaacks left the stand, stopping to shake hands with the Piels on his way out. He smiled at them but looked grim when he left.

With the jury still absent from the courtroom, Hagen then stood and asked the judge to direct the Piels to hand over the report.

"There is no report," Cary Piel said. "There is no report. Donaghue has told me there is no report. Debra Bender and Tony Paul have told me there is no report. Lee Ann Breading has told me there is no report. There is no report."

———

There was a sense in the courtroom that the state's case was winding down.

On Tuesday, Susan Piel led several more of Viki's colleagues through testimony about what a fine teacher and doting mother she'd been and their suspicions about her husband.

Cheryl Seiber testified that she'd worked with Viki at Hodge Elementary School. She remembered a time when a group of teachers and their husbands all went out to eat at a Mexican restaurant. Waiters set out bowls of chips and small cups of hot sauce.

"Viki went to reach for a chip and [Bobby] stopped her with his hand," she said. "He said that will make you fat. She put her hands in her lap. That was an awkward moment."

Whitney Gohlke was next on the stand. Viki was very thin, she testified. But she worried constantly about her weight. If she thought she had gained an ounce she would "over exercise."

The other teachers didn't really like Bobby coming to school. Their own husbands never came, and it wasn't like Bobby was anxious to see her; it was that he wanted to control her. "It was about what he brought for her to eat. He brought her sugar-free candy for Valentine's Day."

Chris Kerner was emotional when she spoke of her friend and fellow schoolteacher. She cried when she saw a photo of Viki holding her young son. Viki had had a passion for teaching and a love for children, she said.

"I asked her once, when are you going to have children? She didn't even answer me and she went over to a cabinet and got her purse and pulled out a picture. I didn't even recognize her. She was fat in the picture. [Bobby] made her carry that picture around," Kerner said, her voice breaking. "He weighed her at the gym. She dreaded getting on that scale."

After a few more witnesses who spoke of plans Viki was making in her last days of life, the state rested.

Hagen had no questions for any of them. He likely knew better than to try to discredit a teacher.

CHAPTER 22

THE DEFENSE CASE

On Wednesday, July 29, 2009, defense attorney Rick Hagen's "second chair," the young attorney Sarah Roland, carried the Lozanos' bed in alone, piece by piece. Hagen, private investigator Kenny Wilson and defense witness Lawrence Renner apparently had more pressing issues to handle. Roland carried in the frame, the box spring and finally the plastic-wrapped mattress while the three men conferred. Denton Police evidence room techs hauled in boxes and garbage bags full of bulky looking items. The defense case appeared to have a lot of props involved.

Finally, Hagen looked over, observed Roland's difficulty in putting the bed together and told Bobby to help her. The spectators were fascinated. What on earth did he plan? Maybe this finally was going to be the day Hagen pulled a rabbit out of his hat.

When the judge was settled in his seat, before he called in the jury, Roland approached with a motion. She had done some legal research. She cited case law and a case that had some similarity to the issue with Dr. Edmund Donaghue. She had a certified copy of Bruce Isaacks's affidavit indicating that Donaghue had written a statement saying Viki's death was a suicide and that Dr. Gary Sisler had then changed his mind and also ruled the death a suicide. She wanted the affidavit entered into evidence.

Cary Piel objected.

Judge McFarling took a moment to consider. Then he issued a surprising statement:

"There's an issue of trustworthiness," he said of the former district attorney's sworn statement. "There's a big problem here."

He spoke of Dr. Sisler's testimony, which stated that Dr. Donaghue told him he agreed with the "undetermined" ruling on manner of death and that he'd never varied from the opinion that the manner of death could not be determined simply by using autopsy results.

"That gives me a very, very big question [about whether] another report is out there," he said. "I'm going to sustain the objection and not allow any mention of Dr. Donaghue or that report."

It was clear that the judge did not believe a report existed. It must have been awkward for McFarling, who'd been hired by Isaacks back when he was a young attorney to work as a prosecutor. After several years he had used that job as a springboard to run for state district judge. Now he was essentially saying that he did not believe what Isaacks swore to was the truth.

The next up to the witness stand was Lawrence Renner, among other things a bloodstain analyst. His gray hair was cut in a haphazard way that looked like it had been accomplished with hedge clippers. He had an air of self-pride and dramatic overattention to detail that could only be described as "fusty." He testified for twenty-five minutes to back up his expertise in forensics, gained by a career in various law enforcement and forensic units in New Mexico. Hagen really wanted the jury to believe this man was the last word on evidence.

And he had many words on the Lozano evidence. Renner began by stating that he had extensive experience notifying people that their loved ones had died, and he knew that everyone reacted differently to sudden death. He had reviewed all the reports that described Bobby's demeanor and had read Bobby's statement. He saw nothing at all that indicated that Viki's husband was behaving inappropriately upon her death.

Hagen went through the physical evidence piece by piece, and Renner disagreed with every conclusion others had made. Based on his own review of the evidence, he did not see a substantial amount of oil on the grip of the gun, he said. It was mostly on the slide. He commented on the pair of socks that had been lying on top of the cleaning kit. They were stained with something, he said. It could have been oil. Perhaps Viki had put them on her hands to clean the gun and that accounted for the lack of oil on her hands. He didn't explain how she could have cleaned the gun while wearing what amounted to mittens on her hands, let alone how, if she'd had the socks on her hands when she pulled the trigger, they could have been removed after she died.

Hagen moved on. He took a can of Break-Free oil and sprayed it on one of his hands. He showed it to Renner, who said he could see a slight sheen of oil on his left hand. Then he asked the judge to allow him to let the jurors smell his hand. Cary Piel was out of his seat immediately with an objection. He didn't want jurors sniffing Hagen's hand.

"Your honor, I'm trying to show that she could have had oil on her hands and it dried," Hagen said.

The judge sustained the objection, and Hagen moved on with one oily hand.

He questioned Renner about death. Even death called "instantaneous" isn't really instant, Renner said. It takes moments, even with as severe an injury as Viki had. The body can move, he vowed. It can make both conscious and unconscious movements. And if she moved after the gun fired into her heart, that could have allowed things on the bed to move around. Her hand could have brushed the oilcan, accounting for the bloody fingerprint smudge on the bottom. She could even have sat up, Renner insisted. That kind of movement might account for the way Bobby found her when he walked in.

Renner even had some complicated, technical explanations for the bloodstains that appeared to show the coverlet had been turned down after being against the bottom sheet and the newspaper that had been stained from the bottom.

Then Hagen started opening the evidence boxes and bags brought in by the evidence techs, and the stench of seven-year-old blood began to permeate the courtroom. He brought out, one by one, the sheets, comforter, pillows and electric blanket that had been on the bed the night Viki died. Renner asked for plastic gloves, and a bailiff found a box of them. Renner spread each item of bedding in its turn and pointed out dog hairs. He counted them. He seemed excessively fussy, changing gloves every time he changed items. The gloves became a joke, with spectators smiling or rolling their eyes each time he insisted he needed a new pair. He pulled them off with a flourish.

Twice, Hagen asked jurors to come down from the jury box and gather around the bed with a bloodstained item spread out on it. The first time they looked reluctant. The second time it seemed some of them were going to flatly refuse. The blood was brown and crusty where it had poured from Viki's body. Renner pointed out dog hair after dog hair. Hagen was trying to drive home the dogs-on-the-bed-moving-things-around theory, and he wouldn't stop until he'd shown the jury every piece of material that had been there that night.

During the morning break Hagen produced a large spray can of air freshener, spritzing the jury box thoroughly with it. One of the jurors had complained that the blood stench was making her sick. He sprayed around the defense table but left the prosecution table alone.

Hagen resumed questioning after the break. He lay on the bed, and Renner rolled him over to show how the paramedic looking for lividity or the hearse attendants could have disturbed the items and moved them from place to place. Hagen asked Renner about the lack of blood on Bobby's hands after performing CPR. Most people have an aversion to getting blood on their hands, and Bobby would not have placed his hands directly on the wound, was Renner's explanation.

He testified that if several people had been standing in the bedroom, likely all of them would have gunshot residue on them. It is a fine powder being forced out the end of the gun with great pressure, he said. So it followed that if Bobby's clothes had no gunshot residue, he was not in the room when the gun fired, according to his theory.

He ended his direct testimony with the declaration that there was not enough physical evidence to support the finding of homicide. Police could not even prove that Bobby had been in the room, he said.

Cary Piel rose from his seat to cross-examine with determination in his step and a gleam in his eye. He was ready to take this witness apart.

"If he shot her before he left, he would have been in the room, right?" Piel quickly asked, and Renner demurred.

Piel began questioning Renner about the gun. Renner explained that he knew nothing about guns.

"So, all those times they sent you to crime scenes, they just sent you to shovel murders?" Piel asked sarcastically.

There was a stir in the courtroom. People sensed that this was going to be a battle, and it was going to be interesting.

Piel asked about cleaning the gun. Renner denied any knowledge of how to clean a gun. Piel lay down on the bed. He took the toy pistol he had been using instead of the real Glock and positioned himself the way he said Viki had to have been lying when the gun went off.

"Is pointing a gun at my chest and pulling the trigger part of the cleaning process?" he asked.

"I don't know," Renner said smugly. "I'd have to have a list of the steps in the cleaning process."

Piel stayed on the bed. He spoke of the relative positions of the kit and the oilcan. He referred to this expert witness's theory that Viki might have moved around after her death and brushed her hand against the oilcan, which was some distance away on the bed.

"Did you see in that photo that she was particularly long-armed?" he asked.

"I couldn't say," Renner said.

Piel made himself comfortable on the bed, using it for effect to ridicule Renner as he tried to get him to admit that the force of the bullet would tend to push the body back on the bed, not forward.

"I'm not sure there's enough energy to send you in any direction," Renner retorted.

Now Hagen wanted the bed out of the room. Cary Piel was having too much fun with it.

"You don't want to give Cary a prop like that," Susan Piel said later. "He'll tear you up with it."

Cary laughed. "I lost my mind up there," he joked. "I had Renner by the throat and I was banging his head against the floor and I just couldn't stop."

Susan said she had been out of the courtroom during the first part of Cary's cross-examination. When she walked back in, he was asking the question about shovel murders.

"I leaned back and asked Tracy Murphree, 'Has it been like this the whole time?' He said, 'Pretty much,'" she said, smiling at her husband's ferocity.

With the jury out on a break, Hagen asked that the bed be removed before Anna Farish came in. It would upset her to see the bed, knowing they were demonstrating her daughter's death, Hagen said.

Cary Piel argued that it would be "weird and awkward" to remove the bed with the jury in the courtroom. The bed stayed awhile longer.

After the break Piel resumed questioning Renner. The bullet harmed the heart, stomach, liver and spleen. Death would have been instantaneous. That was the least likely environment for the body to move after the bullet tore through all those vital organs, wouldn't Renner agree?

No, Renner said. Bodies were still capable of moving.

But wouldn't he agree that was extremely unlikely?

"I disagree," the witness said.

"So you're saying [a body] can sit up after death. How many sit-ups do you think [it] would do—five, ten?"

"I cannot answer that," said Renner.

Piel referred to Bobby's statement that Viki was leaning over when he found her, that he tried to pick her up and she fell lifeless on the bed so he called 911. The ambulance arrived in four minutes, the record showed, he said. Lividity should have been in her face if Viki had been in that position when Bobby found her.

"OK, would you agree that it is not possible she could have lividity in four minutes?"

"I cannot agree with that."

Piel began asking rapid-fire questions that Renner avoided giving direct answers to. Again and again, he asked yes-or-no questions that Renner tried to answer in another way.

"Your honor, the witness is being unresponsive. Would you ask him to answer the questions as they are asked?"

The judge did that, but it had little effect on Renner, who was determined to stymie Piel. By this point, it seemed Renner would not have agreed with him that humans need oxygen to breathe.

When the tussle with Renner was finally over, there was another break, and the bed was eventually removed in preparation for the witness everyone had been waiting for: Anna Farish.

———

Anna Farish, Viki's mother, the woman who had allowed Bobby to continue to live with her and to move his girlfriend into the room where her daughter died, was waiting at the door.

She entered the courtroom with her head high, her hair an unlikely rosy reddish brown. She wore a black-and-white suit and a hard expression.

Hagen had her introduce herself to the jury. She taught private piano lessons, she said. Her husband had held a doctorate in performance and voice, and they had met in college. He'd died in 1995, after thirty-three years as a professor at the University of North Texas.

She testified that in 2002 she taught between seventy and one hundred students. She taught mostly in her home, and on Saturdays she taught in a private home in Plano.

Her piano studio was on the driveway side, or south side, of the house. There was a separate entrance there so the students didn't have to come in the front door. Her bedroom suite also was on that side, as was Monty's room. She testified that she left a key under the doormat and that students knew they could enter at any time to practice.

As a child, her daughter, Viki, had been a tomboy, Anna said. She'd played football with her brother, David. Later, she played on a women's softball team. She was good at putting things together, her mother said.

By the time her daughter was four years old, she was too small for her age. Then she had her tonsils removed and gained two dress sizes in two months, Anna said. And she kept gaining weight. She believed her daughter suffered from depression from the time she was ten because of her weight.

Anna said that when Viki was a senior in high school, one of her friends told the guidance counselor that she believed Viki was on drugs. The counselor confronted

Viki, who was devastated. She didn't want to return to that school, ever, her mother testified. So Anna and her husband arranged for Viki to go to live with her grandparents in Arkansas and finish school there, although "Denton High School was kind enough to let her walk across the stage at graduation."

Anna Farish said that the night Viki came home after being accused of drug use, Viki took a bottle of Tylenol. She had to be rushed to the hospital and had her stomach pumped, her mother said.

"Did you not tell me that when Viki attempted suicide it was because her grandmother died?" Piel asked in cross-examination.

No, Anna said stubbornly. "I did not." But she did say that there was a history of suicide in the family.

Later, other relatives refuted that claim, saying there had never been any suicides in the family.

Anna said Viki and Bobby had known each other slightly in high school, but it was after her daughter enrolled at UNT that she ran into him again. Bobby was working at a filling station.

"Viki was totally impressed with his body. He had been a skinny little thing in high school, and he had become all muscled up. They started working out together," Anna Farish said. "She was a lonely girl when he came into her life, and she was happy that he cared enough to help her with her weight problem."

Anna also insisted that her daughter was familiar with guns. "Viki had a gun at one point, and she was such a good shot." Anna said that she had previously seen Viki clean a gun while sitting on her bed. "I would go in many times and I would see a newspaper on the bed and the cleaning kit and socks. I never actually saw her cleaning a gun but she did."

Anna also said that she'd once seen Viki and Bobby together cleaning his service pistol at the kitchen table. "I told them not to do it there because we had so many students in the house. They said they would clean it back in their bedroom," she testified.

She reinforced the idea of the dogs jumping on the bed that night.

"Many times I've been on my bed with a Coke in my hand and the five dogs have jumped on my bed and bumped me and knocked the Coke out of my hand and I had to change my sheets," she declared.

Bobby and Viki had a wonderful marriage, according to Anna. Monty "was born and bred in a lot of love." Viki planned to be a mother again, she said. That was one reason she was taking the year off from school. She was also planning Monty's first birthday party, which would have been the next month.

Anna Farish cried for the first of only two times during her testimony when she told the jury that "there was the greatest love between them I've ever seen."

Judge McFarling ordered a break, and while jurors were out, a video screen was set up in front of them. It was to show home video Bobby had taken of the baby. Monty was getting his first bath, and Bobby's voice-over was telling Viki what to do.

"You need to go jogging," the dad told his two-month-old baby. "You have a big ol' belly."

The dogs could be heard on the video barking in the room. Renee Lozano left the courtroom and didn't return until the video was over.

It went on and on. Now it showed Viki on a horse with Monty. Now it was Viki and the baby laughing. The video went on for nearly an hour, when Bobby's voice suddenly broke through.

"Say Daddy," he told his tiny son. "Dad-dy. That's the only word you ever have to remember. You don't even have to worry about Mommy."

Gasps went up from the women in the courtroom. What on earth had the defense been thinking, introducing that video with that little scene on it? Perhaps whoever put together the program hadn't been paying attention; or perhaps no one watched it prior to introducing it at all.

Anna Farish had been sitting in a chair between the jury and the screen during the show. When it was finally over, she moved back to the witness stand.

After Monty was born, both Viki and Bobby increased their life insurance to a million dollars, Anna said. Bobby didn't induce his wife to do it. It was Viki's idea.

Anna also refuted most of her own previous statements. She testified that she'd never told Lieutenant Lee Howell to close the investigation and declare the death an accident.

"I told him to find out the truth, which is all I ever

wanted," she said. "I wanted to find out what happened to my daughter."

She said she was insulted by Howell's treatment of her. He asked a lot of questions, as though he were interviewing her. She thought he was rude.

"I didn't feel like I was treated like the mother of someone who has passed."

Viki's mother told the jury that the police would not release any information about her daughter's death to her. She cried as she described the impolite treatment she said she received.

"I couldn't believe that as a mother I didn't have the right to the truth."

———

After Rick Hagen passed the witness, prosecutor Susan Piel took over. Hers was a ticklish situation. She had to show up Anna Farish's obvious contradictions without appearing to attack the mother of the victim. She'd never been in a position like that before. Few prosecutors ever were—mothers of victims were usually prosecution witnesses, holding up a photo of their children and crying about how much the victim was missed. There had been none of that with Anna. Instead, she'd been a hostile witness for the prosecution. But despite Anna's antagonism, Piel knew she still had to confront her in only the most nonconfrontational way.

Did Viki go out much? Piel began.

She went to work, of course. She went to work out, her

mother said. But mostly, she conceded, Viki stayed at home.

Did Bobby control what she ate?

"She would ask him—she would say, 'I can't control how many potato chips I'm eating. Would you remove the bag?' He only took things away from her when she asked him."

Anna denied ever having told Piel's assistant that Bobby was often away from home on weekends and holidays because he was called out from work. She also claimed not to have known that her son-in-law was having an affair. Later, however, during redirect from Hagen, Anna testified that Viki had become suspicious that her husband was having an affair when she was paying the telephone bill and found a number of calls to one telephone number that she wasn't familiar with. Obviously, Anna and Viki thought it was the number of a paramour.

Susan Piel asked Anna about how she'd told Lieutenant Lee Howell that she'd once listened to a telephone message Bobby mistakenly left on the house phone that she believed was meant for another woman. Did she remember telling Lieutenant Howell that she watched Bobby like a hawk after that?

No, she said. She never said that either. She also denied telling Howell that only a determination of accidental death was acceptable.

Anna Farish testified she'd never heard anything about a divorce. She knew nothing about Bobby renting an apartment. She said he didn't tell her that he went to his girlfriend's house in the early morning hours to end the affair, as she'd earlier told the prosecution he did.

She admitted that Bobby and his new wife now lived with her. But she insisted that Renee never had blond hair despite plenty of photographic evidence to the contrary on the Lozanos' own real estate website. Renee's hair was silvery blond in those photos.

Piel continued to go through Anna Farish's previous statements, and Anna slashed each one. "You didn't tell me that he said he washed his hands after he did CPR before picking the baby up?"

No.

"Isn't it true that after Viki's death [Bobby] traded in her SUV and got himself a BMW?"

No.

"He saved her life," Anna Farish blurted out.

Susan Piel passed the witness. Rick Hagen did a little testimony mending. Why was Viki cremated? There was a columbarium in their church, and Viki's father had been cremated and his ashes placed there. Viki had said she wanted to be with her father, Anna Farish said.

She left the stand, and the judge dismissed the jury for the day, leaving spectators to wonder whether Hagen had any more witnesses up his sleeve.

Court was already full half an hour before it was set to reconvene on Thursday, July 30, 2009.

But the day was an anticlimax.

Defense attorney Rick Hagen rose when the judge seated himself. "Your honor, the defense rests," he said.

Judge Bruce McFarling looked at prosecutor Cary Piel. He had but one witness on rebuttal, and that was the Texas Ranger. Tracy Murphree sat again on the witness stand. Recently, Murphree said, he had worked with UNT forensics expert Ed Hueske. They had taken Cindy Waters's statement and followed her movements on the day Viki died. She had a firm alibi, the Ranger said. They could prove everything she said she'd done and where she'd been when Viki died.

"She was eliminated as a suspect."

The state rested and closed. The defense closed. Judge McFarling told jurors that they had heard all the evidence they were going to hear in the case. He instructed them to return at 8:30 A.M. on Friday.

CHAPTER 23

FINAL ARGUMENTS

During the first week of the trial, my friend Sherry DeBorde had been in Chicago on business, though she'd often called me to find out what was happening in court. As soon as she'd returned, however, she'd become a fixture at the trial from then on, just as hooked as everyone else on the drama unfolding in the 362nd District Court.

We'd dissect testimony over hurried lunches then would rush back to the courthouse. It was getting harder and harder to find a seat every day. That Thursday, I wrote a shorter-than-usual story for the next day's edition of the *Record-Chronicle*. Then I fell like a stone onto my couch and slept for the whole afternoon.

When Friday, July 31, 2009 dawned, I was suddenly terrified that I wouldn't be able to get a seat in the court-room. Everyone wanted to hear summations, and courtrooms were traditionally full on those days even for murder trials that were not as high-profile as this one. Sherry and I had agreed to meet at the courthouse at 7:30 A.M. That's when the doors were unlocked. But I was afraid that wouldn't be early enough. I called Sherry, and she shared my fears. We walked up to the front of the courthouse at 7:10 and took our places in a line that was already about twenty people long. The first person in line said he'd arrived at 6:30 A.M.

I stood in my high heels for the hour and twenty minutes while the line grew ever longer behind me. I told Sherry that we were not likely to fit into the first set of two elevators that would be boarding for the third floor. I suggested we take the stairs. She agreed. At 7:30 A.M. a guard unlocked the two front doors. We lined up to pass through the metal detectors, and then Sherry and I rushed for the stairs. People were streaming across the lobby, some following us and some heading for the elevators. Halfway up the stairs to the third floor, we both were wondering if we'd really had the best idea. I hadn't run up three flights of stairs in years, and I was out of breath. But we reached the courtroom door at the same time as the first elevator full of people bound for the courtroom.

There were new rules today. The bailiffs handed each of us a bright red card. That was our ticket into the courtroom, they said. We still would not be allowed back in if the call of nature was too insistent during final arguments. But for breaks, the red card was our ticket back into the courtroom. I sighed in relief. I knew I would not have been able to allow myself a bathroom break, and now I could make myself comfortable knowing I would get my seat back after an announced break.

Once settled in her seat, one woman then started out. You can leave, the bailiff told her, but someone else will be given your seat. But it's only 8 A.M., she said. Court won't even take up for thirty more minutes.

"The game has begun," he said. And she walked slowly back to her seat.

CHAPTER 24

THE CHARGE

The courtroom was full by 8 A.M., and the crowd waited impatiently for the main actors in the play. Finally, the prosecutors were settled on their side of the aisle, and the defense team sat tensely at their table. The judge called for the jury to be seated in their box, and then McFarling read the charge, the law governing what a jury can and cannot do when deciding a verdict. This one included the option for jurors to find Bobby guilty of murder, manslaughter, criminally negligent homicide, or find him not guilty. Presumably Rick Hagen had insisted that the lesser charges be included, as they usually drew considerably shorter sentences than murder. If the defense attorney could convince the jury to go for a lesser charge and assess less than ten years for a sentence, his client had a chance for probation.

It was always tough to anticipate what a jury was going to do.

The courtroom was quiet, despite the mass of people squeezed into the pews. Jurors seemed to sense the tension in the room. They sat straight in their chairs. Some leaned forward. Bobby Lozano's face was unreadable. His wife Renee looked fragile and terrified and somehow already defeated though she was supported by a long row of nieces and nephews, along with Bobby's brothers and his sister and her retired judge husband.

Prosecutor Susan Piel began her summation. She started through the evidence against Bobby, comparing it to his statement and showing his lies. She pointed out his "crazy June" when it looked as though he'd lost Cindy Waters and the pressure was mounting. She spoke with disdain about the supplemental statement Hagen had brought to the police.

"He tells them in his statement that he and Viki fell asleep together the night of their anniversary. He forgets to mention that he went to Cindy's house for two hours."

On Monday after Viki's death, Bobby called Cindy to find out if she had told anyone about their relationship.

"At the exact time he's writing up that statement, Cindy is with Lieutenant Howell singing like a bird," Piel said. "When he calls her, she tells him, 'I told them everything.' Did she tell them about the 'D'? he asked, meaning the divorce. 'Everything,' she said.

"He knows Cindy has talked and he has to go in there and cover it up."

So Bobby told his lawyer, and Hagen brought in the half-page supplement that said he had not talked about his two hours with Cindy that night because he hadn't wanted to admit he was having an affair.

He had more than one reason to want Viki dead. There was the million-dollar insurance policy, Susan Piel pointed out.

Piel sarcastically talked about the parts of Bobby's statement where he claimed he and Viki spent hours at the park that day. There was no one to dispute that story, but it didn't hold up to scrutiny. What must Viki's attitude have been like toward him when Bobby returned home after being "at the office" for two hours? Was she really going to drive off to the park with him, knowing he'd cheated on her? Wasn't it considerate of him to wait until midnight so that it wouldn't technically still be his anniversary night? And how much sleep had he gotten after he arrived home?

"With four hours' sleep and the baby sick they go to the park," she said incredulously.

Bobby said he'd steam cleaned their bedroom that afternoon while the baby slept.

"He cleaned the room at some point, but not then," Piel said, insinuating that he'd cleaned up the room after Viki's death, cleaned his wife's blood off the carpet and staged the scene as best he could to look like an accident had happened while his wife lay dead on their bed.

Bobby claimed to have played a computer game for an hour before starting to clean the gun. Jim Willingham had told jurors the computer was not used during that time, she reminded them. Bobby was trying to account for time to blur the exact moment when Viki died.

Susan Piel ridiculed the gun cleaning on the bed.

"'Oh, I need to stop and leave all this stuff because I had an emergency tanning session because I have not tanned since yesterday.' He just shot his wife and he needs an alibi," she said.

Just as ridiculous, she said, was the idea that Viki would commit suicide. "I think I'm going to kill myself and leave the baby that I've waited sixteen years for alone in the house."

Everyone who saw Bobby that night described him as making crying noises but never shedding a tear.

"He is selfish. He is a liar. He is a master manipulator," she said.

After Susan Piel sat down, defense attorney Sarah Roland, Hagen's young lawyer assistant, stood up. Roland was slim and pretty, with long blond hair—apparently just Bobby's type—but until this point she had been given only menial jobs to carry out and had spent most of her time setting up electronics for Hagen and handing him things. But now, she was to have a few moments in front of the jury.

"I don't get it," she began, sounding like a prosecutor instead of a lawyer trying to convince a jury to find her client innocent. "Why would Viki stay with him? Why would Cindy stay with him? I don't know. Why would anyone with any self-worth stay? He is apparently God's gift to women. A little bit of sweet talk and they're back

with him. . . . [He tells Viki,] 'I've got to go to the office,'"
she said. "You think she doesn't know where he's going?"

Roland talked about the home videos, evidence presented by the defense.

"How much was Viki not in the picture? It's just Bobby
and Monty, talking about how fat the baby is—taking a
jab at Viki. That's how her life is. She barely even talks.
She's not happy. He says, 'I'm going to tan.' Why should
she believe that? Then what?"

And tossing her long hair around, Roland sat down.
Throughout her summation, spectators had been expecting the "but." Bobby was a jerk to his wife "but" . . .
However, Roland had stopped short of the "but." Presumably, Roland was trying to show Viki's hopelessness and
make a case that Viki had committed suicide; yet truthfully, she couldn't have done a better job of prosecuting
Bobby had she stood in front of the prosecution table. It
was weak at best.

Roland had taken only a few minutes, leaving the rest
of the time allotted for final arguments to Rick Hagen. He
began by reminding jurors that the manner of death still
was considered "undetermined" on the autopsy report.
Then he tried a strange tactic. He accused Cary Piel of
having insulted Dr. Gary Sisler, the pathologist, by calling
him "Pops."

"Because he did not agree with their theory, they had
to disrespect him," Hagen said.

Then he told the jury that they could create a set of
facts that made Bobby guilty.

"You can think it. You can believe it. You can be clearly

convinced that it's true," he said. "But they have to prove it beyond a reasonable doubt."

The lawyer went all through the shell casing argument again. No document, no report in the whole case ever said that the shell casing was found under the cleaning kit, he reminded jurors. The report of the detective writing the evidence log showed the shell casing listed above the cleaning kit and the newspaper, which Hagen said proved that it was found first.

"If they can prove beyond a reasonable doubt that the shell casing never moved, then you can convict Bobby Lozano," he said.

Alternatively, he suggested that the paramedic who "rolled" the body might've dislodged the shell casing and caused it to roll under the kit. Or, he suggested, the men who moved Viki's body to the gurney might have dislodged the shell casing. Or maybe it was the dogs' fault, and they had dislodged the shell casing and it rolled under the kit.

Hagen discussed the 911 tape. Was it enhanced to determine whether the baby's cries or Bobby's pleas for Viki not to leave them might become audible? In times of stress, things become distorted, he said.

"He says [in his statement] that he was begging her not to die, but was he only thinking it?"

Refuting all the testimony from Viki's colleagues, Hagen said that however she might've presented herself at work, she was not a happy woman.

He spoke of Anna Farish. She had told them, he said to the jury, that she'd asked Bobby and Viki to move their gun-cleaning operation out of the kitchen.

"Why is Anna Farish going to come in here and make that up?" he asked.

And Anna had only pressed for an accidental finding because she did not want to admit that her daughter killed herself.

"You are required to presume Bobby Lozano is innocent despite the hate you feel for him," Hagen said. "Make them prove beyond a reasonable doubt that it was not a suicide, not an accident. Do the right thing."

Cary Piel stood up and walked over to the jury box. Gone was the fiery prosecutor who had challenged and ridiculed the defense expert witness. Gone was the wicked wit he had used in opening statements. Piel leaned over the witness box with his hands out beside him. He spoke so quietly that spectators had a hard time hearing him. Piel didn't care about that. He was talking to the jury. Looking them in the eye. Speaking to each one, individually. Softly. Convincingly.

The defense was misleading them, he said.

"No matter how slowly, how ponderously it is said, over and over, that is not the way you do it," Piel said. "You only have to prove the elements of the crime beyond a reasonable doubt."

Remember how ludicrous Lawrence Renner was as a witness, he told them. "That sense of silliness. . . . How ludicrous it was that he spends twenty-five minutes talking about his credentials to make him sound important. And he isn't. His testimony was ludicrous."

There was no reasonable belief that a dog caused Viki to shoot herself or that she committed suicide while lying in that position on her side, he said. "That is ludicrous."

As for Dr. Sisler, "Pops" was a term of affection for a man he respected, Piel told them. To accuse him of disrespecting the doctor was "ludicrous."

The difference in the photographs had been fully explained. The officers took many photos to document the process of removing things from the bed. Of course they were different, Piel said quietly. They were taken at different stages of the evidence recovery.

Then Cary Piel moved on to Bobby Lozano himself.

"This man—we're going to talk about him negatively now. His character is beyond anything normal. If he came in and his beloved wife was dead on that bed, he should have held her. But he didn't, because there is no blood on him. He lives in that same bedroom where he killed her.

"What a life she had with those two," Piel said, referring to Anna Farish and Bobby Lozano. "But it was finally better. She had a baby who loved her."

What would Bobby have lost, had he divorced Viki? he asked. He would have lost the money. He would have lost the house he'd designed himself. He would have lost the freedom to run around. Bobby loved himself more than he loved anyone else.

"She bled in that bed, and she died in that bed. This nice lady who loved that baby. How many milestones has she had taken from her because he couldn't keep his business in his pants?

"It's been long enough," Cary Piel said. "It's time for justice for this nice lady."

It was quiet in the courtroom as Piel walked back to the prosecutor's table and sat down. Then Judge McFarling sent the jury to the jury room to deliberate. It was 10:30 A.M. on the last day of July 2009.

CHAPTER 25

—•—

WAITING

No one from the gallery left the courtroom. People kept asking me how long it would take for the jury to deliberate, as though I had a secret window into the jury room. I had no idea.

The judge went to his chambers, and the bailiffs went behind the doors to rooms and offices. The prosecutors went to their offices across the hall, and the defense team vacated the courtroom as well. The spectators lined the benches, whispering at first, and then gradually becoming louder as they relaxed for the wait. No one could guess how long it could be.

Sherry left and found us some tacos. We ate them in the lobby of the third floor. I talked briefly to Jeff Wawro, who was waiting out the jury too. I walked the hallways. Every few steps, as in the weeks before, someone stopped me to thank me for bringing the case back to the courthouse. I was a little embarrassed by the praise. But I couldn't deny my part. I was proud of it.

We finally went back into the courtroom and found seats. The benches still were full. People were laughing, telling stories, joking. They were reading books and magazines. One woman was knitting. A couple of folks were playing games on their smartphones. I could see them sneaking bites of candy and chips from their handbags and stealing sips of water or soft drinks from concealed bottles. The bailiffs weren't in the courtroom, and the time was getting long. A slight lapse of courtroom decorum prevailed.

Then a bailiff poked a head into the courtroom from the hallway outside the jury room. I sensed her excitement. I knew what was coming. A stir went through the room, and the prosecutors and defense lawyers walked back in. Bobby and Renee emerged from the anteroom where they had been waiting. He took his seat, his face expressionless. Renee began to cry even before the jury walked back in.

As the ten women and two men filed back into the jury box, I looked at them. The women were mostly young females, not unlike the women Bobby had wooed in the past. But Bobby had lost some of the glamour he affected seven years ago. He wasn't quite as buff, not quite as polished. His face was lined, and he'd had no chance to show them his old-world courtliness. Perhaps they wondered what the women in Bobby's life had seen in him.

Judging by one of the men's expressions during testimony, I suspected that he had begun to hate Bobby by the time Cindy finished her testimony. The other man apparently had no sympathy for Bobby's lothario ways either.

The two rows of family sat tensely, some holding hands. Tricia, Frank Lozano's wife, put her arm around Renee.

The bailiff handed the judge the jury's written decision.

"We the jury," McFarling intoned, "find the defendant guilty of murder."

Bobby was perfectly still. Behind him, Renee slowly lowered her head as tears flooded her face and her shoulders began to shake. Tricia held her tighter. Bobby turned and walked to her. But the bailiffs gestured to him and led him back to a holding cell. He was in custody. Renee broke completely down, sobbing, as family members tried to comfort her. They were crying too.

I watched as Bobby Lozano's relatives left the courtroom. The women were crying, and the men had their arms protectively around them. Anna Farish wasn't there. Except for the time she spent on the witness stand, she'd stayed at home. Bobby's parents never came to the courthouse. His father was dying, and his mother remained at his father's side. Did they even understand what was happening?

I felt like a voyeur, but I needed to see. I had to report it to my readers. They wanted to know. It was not just the verdict they wanted; it was the emotion. And there was plenty of it in the courtroom. I moved outside and took a seat on a bench. I watched as the family led Renee down the hallway, holding her up as she almost fell. Renee, I thought. Renee, the woman who'd used Bobby's name but whom he'd married only two weeks before the trial began. The woman who would be raising his child, if she stayed.

In the comments under one of my articles, there had been a message for Renee from a woman who said she was Bobby's current mistress. She had been in the courtroom, she said. She believed he was guilty. "Run, Renee, run," she wrote.

Renee was another one of Bobby's victims.

My telephone started ringing before I even left the courthouse. Everyone wanted to congratulate me and thank me and find out how the family took the news. I was numb. I believed that Bobby had murdered his wife. I believed he should pay for that crime. I believed the jury had done the right thing. But when I tried to visualize him sitting in a cell in the county jail, waiting to see what the jury would decide to do with him, I couldn't. I went home and wrote my story, interrupted every few minutes by another telephone call or text message. I went to bed early. But I couldn't sleep.

I hadn't written that first investigative story for the accolades. And somehow, I felt guilty for receiving them. One thing I knew: Without the hard work of those investigators, without the help of Lee Howell in writing that story and without the superb job of prosecuting by Susan and Cary Piel, this conviction would not have taken place.

CHAPTER 26

SENTENCING

On Monday, August 3, 2009, Cary Piel rested the state's case in the punishment phase without calling a witness. This would have been the time to bring forward other bad acts of the defendant or present his pen pack, or penitentiary package, with other convictions had he had any. But he had been a police officer. His record was spotless. He had no prior convictions to point out. The Piels chose not to bring any more of his girlfriends to the stand. Jurors had heard enough of that.

For the first time, Bobby's brother Javier was in the courtroom. He had been the one who sat by himself with a stunned look on his face the night of Viki's death. He sat between his sister, Blanca, and his brother Frank, but he barely spoke to either of them. They talked around him as he sat like a stone.

Javier's presence made it seem that perhaps he would be

put on the witness stand by the defense to ask for mercy for Bobby. Someone had to ask. It was the way a defense worked. Bobby's parents had not been in the courtroom at all. His father's health was precarious, and presumably no one wanted his mother to have to go through such an ordeal.

But it was Frank Lozano, the police officer at the University of North Texas, who took the stand to ask for mercy on his brother's behalf. He stated his name and credentials. He'd been a police officer for twenty-one years. I knew that he must realize his brother's guilt now. He'd sat through the whole trial. He was in law enforcement. He heard the evidence. Still, Bobby was his baby brother.

"Are you here today asking this jury for leniency for your brother?" Hagen asked.

"Yes, sir, I am," Frank Lozano replied.

Cary Piel had only a couple of questions for him.

What kind of home did Bobby grow up in? A very good home, Frank said. Are your parents still together? Yes, they were. Did you know about his running around?

"No, sir, I didn't," Frank replied.

And Cary said that was all and sat down.

Hagen offered Bobby's personnel file into evidence. Then the defense rested.

Renee sat with Bobby's nieces close around her. Her head was bowed, and their arms were around her shoulders. She looked defeated and exhausted.

After a break, final arguments began.

Cary Piel went first this time. Sometimes, it's hard to know where to start, he told the jury. Perhaps they could begin by trying to decide where this crime fit in the hierarchy of murder. There was murder that took place during a drug deal gone wrong. Murder that happened between two criminals. There was spur-of-the-moment, angry killing, and there was premeditated, planned killing.

They should compare the way this murder was done with others and decide where it fell, he advised them. They should consider what kind of man Bobby was and how he lived his life.

"This man—this is almost as bad as killing your own child," he said quietly. "It's as bad as it gets. He ambushed a woman in her bed."

"It was not possible to measure this loss," he said.

"You think of dying and you want to die old, with your children gathered around you, and you say, 'I'm ready.' That's the way it's supposed to happen."

Cary Piel sat down, and Rick Hagen stood. Bobby Lozano had spent sixteen years honorably serving the public as a police officer, he told the jurors.

"He was dedicated, diligent and respected for sixteen years. He was a commended officer. He volunteered as a counselor at camps for schoolchildren. There is more to Bobby Lozano than just this case," he said.

Hagen talked of the tremendous responsibility jurors had to make the right decision. It was easy to argue in a murder case that a life was worth a life, he said. But they could not do it that way. He closed by reminding them of the Bible story of a murderer whom the Lord looked at and forgave.

Susan Piel took over for the final word. She counted the

victims in the case. Bobby betrayed his fellow officers, she said. He brought shame on his department and his brother officers. Jeff Wawro was working that night because it was Bobby's turn to be on call, but Bobby had had something else to do. Wawro then had to investigate the thing that Bobby had to do.

Bobby's family members were victims, she said. They came every day to support him. They listened in shame to the reports of his actions.

"His mother did not raise him to be that hateful, selfish person," she said. His mother-in-law, Anna Farish, believed in him. She loved her grandson, and to turn on Bobby would be to lose the boy.

"If she is ever able to accept what happened, she will be devastated," Susan Piel said.

And there was Monty, nearly eight years old, who only had pictures of his mother and no memories of the woman who had loved him so much. He would celebrate his eighth birthday in twelve days, on August fifteenth.

And Viki, she said, the ultimate victim, who was not even allowed to celebrate one birthday with her son.

"He made a vow till death do you part. He treated her horribly until he executed her," Susan said. "Tell him what you think of that."

The jury left the courtroom to deliberate Bobby's sentence at 9:40 A.M.

───────

While they were out, Cary Piel had some business to take care of with the judge. He said he wanted to bring prosecutor Tony Paul to the witness stand to testify in the ongoing speedy trial motion. Rick Hagen protested and continued to object, but Judge McFarling agreed to hear the testimony.

Paul had been "second chair" in the first case against Bobby, the one that had ultimately been dismissed because of the affidavit signed by the district attorney at the time, Bruce Isaacks. Paul testified that he had full access to all the reports. He traveled to Dallas one Saturday and met the Chicago pathologist, Dr. Edmund Donaghue, at a hotel. They spoke briefly about the case.

"Was there a written report generated in any form or fashion?" Piel asked Paul.

"No. It would have gone through me."

"Did he say to you that he thought it was suicide?"

"No, he did not."

Hagen then asked that the entire state's file be marked and sealed for records purposes for his motion. Piel objected. There is nothing in the file pertaining to this issue, he said. The file was contained in seven boxes. To copy the whole file would be ridiculous. He already had turned over notes from Debra Bender, who'd been the "first chair" prosecutor on the case. Tony Paul wrote no notes on the issue.

Hagen insisted that he needed any notes from any district attorney employee relating to the issue of Dr. Donaghue.

"All notes relating to this issue were turned over to them," Piel insisted. "I'm not giving him my work product!"

"He is hamstringing my ability to cross-examine!" Hagen shot back.

McFarling denied Hagen's request.

_____

At 11:05 A.M., the jury walked back into the courtroom. They had made up their minds.

The forewoman handed the piece of paper to the bailiff, who gave it to the judge.

"We the jury, having found the defendant guilty of murder, now sentence him to forty-five years in prison and additionally assess a ten-thousand-dollar fine," McFarling read. Juries normally don't assess the fines available to them as part of sentences. People in prison have no way to make money, they reason. Perhaps the fine was part of a compromise in the jury room. Perhaps jurors reasoned that Anna Farish would be the one to pay and wanted that. That reasoning never was revealed.

McFarling dismissed the jury. It was over.

Because murder is a "3G" offense, a violent felony, it meant that Bobby would have to stay in prison until any "good time" he accrued and the years he served added up to half of the forty-five years, at which time he could first be considered for parole.

Bobby Lozano left the courtroom for the holding cell with barely a look at his wife Renee, who was crying quietly. The spectators sat as though they expected more to happen. But it was done.

CHAPTER 27

THE AFTERMATH

I left the courtroom and talked to Susan and Cary Piel in the hallway. They were elated at the win. Fox 4 News was there, and the cameraman shot video of everyone leaving the courtroom. I got my share of hugs and thanks as teachers, friends and people who simply wanted to see the end walked by me.

Richard Ray, the Fox 4 newsman, walked out of the courtroom and said the family had no comment and asked to be left alone. I am not a vulture. I honored that request.

They left in small groups, the nieces clinging to their husbands, David White and Blanca looking neither left nor right as they walked to the elevators. I thought about the statement Blanca made the night Viki died; the statement that had shocked Richard Godoy. "We only get one shot at life and you have to take it," she'd told her brother with his dead wife still in her bloody bed. I wondered if Blanca knew more than she was telling. If Bobby had needed help that night, it was compelling to imagine that he might have turned to his sister. But there was absolutely no evidence of that.

I watched as Javier Lozano left the courtroom alone and walked down the hall. He had loved his little brother, but he had also cared about Viki. He still had the stunned, set look on his face and he spoke to no one as he left. I had known him for many years—he'd worked with my husband at a truck plant before my husband died, and before Javier had established his small gym. Both my friend Sherry and I had worked out there, and he'd been fun to train with and generous with his help if you had a problem. I wondered if the happy-go-lucky, laid-back guy I'd known would ever return.

Renee came out crying quietly and left quickly. She, I thought again, was another of Bobby's victims. And she might not even know it yet. But judging from the looks on her face during the trial, I thought she had learned a great deal about her new husband. None of it would tend to keep her waiting forty-five years until he was free.

The next day Sheriff Benny Parkey called me. He'd been out of town most of the week because his son was gravely ill. Still, he called most days to find out what had happened in court that day. He'd ordered that Bobby be moved down to Huntsville that same day, he mentioned.

Why so quickly? I wanted to know.

"It's a crazy little thing called liability."

Police officers' lives are always in jeopardy when they are incarcerated. Parkey didn't want anything to happen to Bobby on his watch. Bobby was transported that day to the Byrd Unit of the Texas prison system, the Texas Department of Criminal Justice. He would remain there at the unit, which was a diagnostic center, until state authorities decided the best placement for him.

A month later I was sitting in a conference room on the lowest sublevel of the Federal Emergency Management Agency building on the east side of town. I was waiting to interview the new national FEMA director, and he was late.

A pretty blond woman stuck her head in the door and smiled at me. Then she walked in and shook my hand.

"You don't know me, but I know you," she said. "Viki Lozano gave my kids piano lessons, and my son was in her fifth-grade class. I was at the trial one day. I'm the one who stopped you and thanked you for getting this started. It never would have happened if you hadn't cared. Thank you."

I smiled as I thought of all the people who had stopped me and thanked me in those halls. All the telephone calls and e-mails I had received. I had thought Viki had had no one to love her, no one to remember that she had died in her bed in her pajamas with yellow ducks on them.

I had been wrong. So many people cared, and so many were proud that Viki finally had her justice.

It was over. And still, one loose strand dangled from the case. Former DA Bruce Isaacks, under oath, had twice testified to something that obviously wasn't true.

Isaacks had sworn in an affidavit to the judge, when he asked that the indictment against Bobby Lozano be dropped, that two medical examiners had determined that Viki Lozano committed suicide. Both doctors, each also under oath, disputed ever having said that.

It bothered me. And it bothered the public. They kept asking me, when was somebody going to do something about Bruce Isaacks and his apparent lying under oath?

I didn't know. I kept asking officials. They didn't know either.

Jamie Beck, first assistant to DA Paul Johnson, told me the Texas Rangers were looking into a possible perjury charge. I spoke with A. P. Davidson, the Ranger in charge of the case. He was working on it, he said. But he wasn't ready to take it to a grand jury.

Denton lawyer Henry Paine was appointed as special prosecutor for Isaacks's case. He and the Ranger finally took the case to a grand jury in July 2010.

The grand jury declined to indict Isaacks.

Paine said in an interview that day, after the grand jury declined to indict, that he and the Ranger thought that Isaacks truly believed what he swore to. Debra Bender, the young lawyer originally assigned to the case, had had little experience in felony cases and no murder trials under her belt. Isaacks had seen a document he believed the Illinois medical examiner wrote, and he was telling the truth as he knew it under oath, Paine said. Likely it was a document that Bender produced explaining why she believed the case should be dropped.

Isaacks, he said, had been misled.

If what the Ranger's investigation showed was true, Bender had lied to her boss, or maybe there had been a gross misunderstanding. But she didn't break any laws. Isaacks was the one who signed the affidavit and testified in front of McFarling.

The outcome angered many people who believed that Isaacks should have been punished for something. But I was OK with the outcome. Justice had been delayed. But it had not, in the end, been denied.

Two months after Bobby Lozano's conviction, on Friday, October 2, 2009, Judge McFarling denied his motion for a new trial. His new attorney, Gary Udashen, filed an appeal. Either the family was through with Rick Hagen, or he was through with him. Perhaps it was mutual. In any case, Udashen was said to specialize in appeals.

Meanwhile, Bobby Lozano remains incarcerated in the Daniel Unit of the Texas prison system. The Daniel Unit lies in West Texas near Abilene. I was in contact by telephone with a spokesman for the prison system, Jason Clark, who said that Lozano is not in a special unit. He is part of the general population. He sleeps, works and eats with other criminals. Clark said prisoners like Bobby, former police officers convicted in high-profile cases, are moved as far from home as possible so they will not be recognized by other prisoners as police officers. If he received threats or was assaulted, Clark said, he could be taken into protective custody within the prison. But for now, Bobby Lozano was on his own. I suspect he spends his days looking over his shoulder, fearing to recognize someone he once put in this prison. Fearing that someone will recognize him. A prison is not a safe place for a former cop who killed his wife.

EPILOGUE

Saint Andrew Presbyterian Church takes up a city block just west of downtown Denton. It consists of several buildings tied together with covered walkways, stairs and sidewalks, and there are rooms on three levels. It is a beautiful but not a traditional-looking church building.

It was quiet on a Friday afternoon. There were three or four cars in the parking lot, but I could see no one. I had no idea where I needed to go. I walked first one way, down a sidewalk and up a short flight of steps to some double doors. They were locked. I retraced my steps, passing a lovely area with a bench, flowers and statuary that invited me to sit and meditate. But I had a mission. I walked around to the east side of one of the buildings near the parking lot. A sign indicated the office lay that way. I climbed another